Contents

3. Backups 33

4. Installation 39

5. Getting Started 57

6. Creating a Book 111

Quick Start and Easy Reference Series

SUTTON LEISURE SERVICES

COMPUTE! BOOKS
Radnor, Pennsylvania

For Kathy, Jennifer, and Steven.

Editor: Pam Williams Plaut

Cover Design: Anthony Jacobson

Clip art was provided by the indicated publishers specifically for use in this book and may not be copied.

Graphics were produced by a LaserPrinter 8 provided by Star Micronics.

Certain images were created using *ComputerEyes* digitizing equipment provided by Digital Vision.

Some scanned images were created using a *ScanMan* hand scanner provided by Logitech.

10 9 8 7 6 5 4 3 2 1

Library of Congress Cataloging-in-Publication Data

Bixby, Robert
  Quick and easy guide to Ventura publisher / Robert Bixby.
    p.   cm.
  ISBN 0-87455-233-0
  1. Desktop publishing. 2. Ventura Publisher (Computer program)
I. Title.
Z286.D47B56   1990
686.2'25445369—dc20   89-39968
                                                          CIP

COMPUTE! Books, Post Office Box 5406, Greensboro, North Carolina 27403, is a Capital Cities/ABC, Inc. company and is not associated with any manufacturer of personal computers.

7. Power Features   141

8. Ideas   149

Appendices

A. Keyboard Shortcuts   155

B. Menu Selections   161

C. Miscellaneous Codes 165

D. Glossary 171

E. Preliminary Steps 179

F. Graphics and Other Enhancements 183

Index 198

Foreword

Ventura Publisher version 2 provides an unprecedented list of power options to the desktop publisher. When *Ventura Publisher* was introduced, few products were so adept at formatting a stream of type. With its new release, *Ventura Publisher* is now the package of choice for graphics as well.

The only problem with massive power is that it is always accompanied by mind-boggling complexity. *Ventura Publisher* is no exception. Many users, on first starting the program, will throw up their hands in desperation. Nothing is more frustrating than a program that can't be put to use immediately. *Ventura Publisher* doesn't invite a user in and treat a person like a friend. Although it's said to be much more friendly in its new release (it provides cryptic help messages with most dialog boxes), its organization is anything but logical on first glance.

Ventura Publisher is actually easy to understand, once a few important details are explained. You can start using it immediately with a book like COMPUTE!'s *Quick & Easy Guide to Ventura Publisher*. And, more importantly, once you've started using *Ventura Publisher* regularly, this book provides ideas for making a publication interesting to look at, easy to read, and professional in every way.

Everything is here to get you started with *Ventura Publisher* in real-life desktop publishing projects. The author walks you through creating a newsletter and a book. He covers importing art with clip art, digitizers, and scanners. He even provides addresses of some clip art publishers and a brief section covering the use of a popular digitizer and hand scanner.

If you're considering getting started with *Ventura Publisher*, or you're using it but want to push it to the limits of its power, this book can help. It's *the* quick start and reference guide to *Ventura Publisher* version 2.

Acknowledgments

I am grateful for the assistance of many people who helped with material and support in the creation of COMPUTE!'s *Quick & Easy Guide to Ventura Publisher*.

My wife, Kathy, and children, Jennifer and Steven, provided me with the time and understanding.

My editor, Pam Plaut, helped whip the book into shape; thanks also to Claudia Earhart, David Florance, and Editor in Chief at COMPUTE! Books, Stephen Levy.

Star Micronics provided me with the services of a Star Micronics LaserPrinter 8 whose performance throughout was stellar. (Thanks to MeeLin Sit and Nathan Soule.)

Digital Vision was kind enough to loan its *ComputerEyes* digitizing system which proved fast and flexible and produced stunning graphics. (Thanks to John Pratt.)

LOGITECH provided use of the *ScanMan* hand scanner and *PaintShow Plus* software. (Thanks to Betty Skov.)

Nelda Forston and others at Xerox provided technical support.

David English provided scanning assistance and expert advice.

Robin Case, Kim Potts and many others at COMPUTE! and elsewhere provided criticism of the layout and artwork examples.

Chapter 1
Desktop Publishing

Chapter 1
Desktop Publishing

Desktop publishing has been with us for some time. It didn't, strictly speaking, arrive with the laser printer, or the Macintosh, or personal computing. People have been publishing on their desktops ever since the mimeograph was invented, and even before that. Desktop publishing is simply creating a published item with normal tools found around the home or office, and can certainly be extended to include work done on the typewriter, Xerox machine, and spirit duplicator.

The reason most people consider desktop publishing as having begun in the middle 1980s is that desktop publications created after that time were expected to have a higher degree of polish than earlier publications. Anyone can tell the difference between a printed page created with a typewriter and one created with a laser printer. Most can appreciate the difference typeset-quality text makes in the appearance of the page. Modern desktop publishing hardware and software also allow the insertion of figures and highly flexible layout options that give the general appearance of a professionally created document.

Sometimes.

There are other documents that might have benefited from the limitations imposed by a typewriter and a bottle of rubber cement. The extreme power and flexibility of modern desktop publishing tools also unleashes the amateur and (let's say it) the tasteless, like Godzilla released from her long hibernation under the Sea of Japan. Their work would normally fall under the scrutiny of a production manager who would prevent it from seeing the light of day. But since desktop publishers are more or less on their own, there's nothing to prevent them from jamming together a grab bag of fonts and clip art, a maze of rules and dingbats, and calling it "desktop publishing." This sort of thing is apt to give the profession a bad name.

Let's narrow the bounds of desktop publishing a little. Let's say desktop publishing is an art unto itself. Some people are gifted at it, others can create beautiful publications through hard work and attention to detail, and still others are potentially capable, but need some amount of instruction before they can fully express themselves with skill and creativity.

The first rule of desktop publishing is that a publication shouldn't be offensive (unless that's the intent). The next rule is that it should be interesting. The material you publish is your own concern. One would hope that it's important and clearly written, and that you have the right to publish it (either the copyright or the permission of the copyright holder), but that's in the realm of editing. As important as good editing is, it's outside the purview of this book. Readers looking for excellent resources on editing are referred to the *Chicago Manual of Style* and Strunk and White's *Elements of Style*.

The Purpose of This Book

The mission of any book about desktop publishing is first, to teach the software and help the reader achieve a certain level of competence, and second, to instill a few very general, very simple rules to keep the desktop publisher from unintentionally falling overboard.

In this book you will learn how to "drive" *Ventura Publisher*, one of the most popular and powerful desktop publishing packages ever created. The discussion must be kept very narrow in order for this book to live up to the description *Quick & Easy* in the title. Therefore, you'll discover that many items are covered in a quick, step-by-step manner that facilitates rapid learning, but doesn't necessarily explore the nuances of the product. Once you learn the package, you should go back and experiment as much as possible with the

4

features to become familiar with them. If you read through this book from cover to cover, you will emerge competent to create a newsletter and a book with *Ventura Publisher*. You'll learn many formatting and layout features, but by no means will you learn everything there is to know about *Ventura Publisher*. It's much too complicated to learn in just a couple of hundred pages.

Think of this book as a stepping stone and a handy reference. When you become familiar with the program, you'll want to keep this book around for sections that tell in a very simple way how to use some of the less common and more technical capabilities of the product.

There are many aspects of desktop publishing that are far too complex to cover in this book, that have been covered well elsewhere, that are common knowledge, or for other reasons are best left to your private study. After all, this isn't a book on everything you need to know in desktop publishing. It's only a quick start and reference guide to *Ventura Publisher* version 2, so it's best to keep the focus tightly on that subject in the very few pages allowed.

However, there are a couple of very basic matters you should know before venturing into *Ventura Publisher* or any other desktop publishing package. These general topics are touched upon below.

Type

Many people enter desktop publishing without much understanding of the power and usefulness of simple type. If you just want to leave a note for someone, you can express your idea with a pencil and paper. You probably don't spend a lot of time conceptualizing the overall appearance of the note, let alone the shape and form of your letters. If you're like me, your letters are mixed capitals and lowercase, half written in cursive and half printed. Some of my letters look as if they came from another alphabet, on another planet, but generally the context makes my message clear.

If this book were printed the same way, you would quickly tire of decyphering the words and you'd move on to something else. The visual quality of the type would be the crucial factor. Even if the words in this book were guaranteed to deliver money and happiness, a certain amount of resolve would be necessary to wade through it if it were handwritten.

Let's take another example. Wedding and graduation announcements sometimes look as if they were written, but they aren't. They are printed in a beautiful calligraphic typeface (or some other equally graceful typeface) that communicates far more than the date and time of the ceremony. The typeface puts the reader into the spirit of the affair: It will be elegant or businesslike, but above all, it will be formal.

Type has a multitude of variables associated with it. First of all, and probably most familiar, is the concept of the *font*. Elsewhere in this text, *font* is only half-seriously defined as a group of characters that look good together, a little like the cast of *The Misfits*. But generally, the letters have more in common than good looks. They share such features as weight (the thickness of the parts of the letter), contrast (the difference between the thinner parts and the thicker parts), size, and other less obvious things that contribute to their general appearance.

Serifs

The simplest division between kinds of fonts is that a font is either *serif* or *sans serif*. Serifs are the little additional lines that finish off the major strokes of a letter, like the lines that hang at either end of the cross in the capital T. These fonts are generally traditional fonts and they often date from other centuries. Their appeal is that they are "easy on the eyes." Some people say the serif provides a visual cue that tells your eye where to stop interpreting the letter. In any case, the fonts with serifs can be read, even if they are quite small, virtually endlessly.

Sans serif fonts are more modern, some dating to the period between the wars. The headings in this book are printed in a sans serif font. Although their appearance is arresting and instantly recognizable, sans serif fonts can be tiresome when they fill page after page. However, you can use them for body text as long as you provide plenty of white space between columns, in the margins, and between lines. The fact that these fonts are usually "equal-weight"— they are the same thickness throughout—makes the letters look like a plate of spaghetti when the text is jammed too tightly together.

Other Aspects of Type

Whether or not a typeface has serifs is only the most obvious feature of the font. Among the other features that will concern you when selecting a typeface is the height of the capitals, the height of the lowercase letters, the size of the open areas (like the hole in the center of the letter *o*), the depth of the descenders (like the tail on the letter *g*), and many other features. Dimensions of the font are so important because deep descenders and tall capitals will tend to get tangled between the lines. If you don't watch the *leading*—the white space between the lines—the ascenders and descenders will become enmeshed like *Velcro*, which can be very hard to read.

The Page

Pages need to be balanced and readable. You need to provide enough room around the words and between the lines so the reader can easily see what the type says. This has been mentioned, but the temptation to jam as much type on the page as physically possible can be very strong. You must fight it.

Use at most three typefaces in an entire publication. If you can, reduce this to two or even one. If you want to make a joke page with all the fonts available, underlined, overstruck, struckout, subscript, and italic, feel free, but don't expect anyone to take it seriously or read it very carefully.

Be conservative with the typeface and liberal with the white space. Spread things out. Don't be afraid to use boxes, inserts, and call-outs to draw attention to important points. Your readers will thank you and, when tastefully done, such enhancements improve the appearance of a publication.

7

Components of a *Ventura Publisher* Publication

A *Ventura Publisher* publication is made up of text and graphics files *poured* into frames on pages. A frame is simply a box you draw on the screen with your mouse pointer. If you don't draw a box on the screen, the page itself is the active frame.

A collection of pages is known as a *chapter*. But don't confuse this term with a chapter in a book. A *Ventura Publisher* chapter can contain one or more individual book chapters. Its only limit is that it can contain no more than 128 individual text and graphic files and it can be no larger than about 500K of text. This is a very generous allotment. 500K is about 300 pages—about the length of an average book. All the text files in this book are barely larger than 200K.

In order to place multiple chapters within a *Ventura Publisher* chapter, you only need to link your chapters end to end as text files. See Chapter 6 for more information about this.

The next larger unit is the *publication*, which can contain multiple chapters.

Within a text file, anything between two carriage returns is called a *paragraph*. A paragraph can be of any length, but it must consist of a single format. The format is called a *tag*. The tag can contain a truly amazing array of options, including a ruling line around the paragraph, justification, extra spacing on any side, special typeface, "drop caps," and so on.

Ventura Publisher also provides the option of adding *graphics* to the text. At one point in this book a certain character will be called for that cannot be created on the keyboard or reproduced by the printer. Instead, it's created as a graphic. The graphic is then anchored to the text in such a way that it is treated like a character: Repositioning the text repositions the graphic. Of course, graphics are a big part of desktop publishing. Graphics can include imported line art from draw programs like *MacDraw*, creations from paint programs like *GEM Paint* or *PC Paintbrush*, rules and guides provided by *Ventura Publisher* itself, clip art (a list of clip art publishers is included in Appendix F), scanned or digitized art, or art created using the draw facilities of *Ventura Publisher*.

Although it has a reputation of not being "good with graphics," *Ventura Publisher* is surprisingly flexible. You can create frames or graphics that appear on each page, for instance. If you have need for a kind of graphic that isn't supported by *Ventura Publisher*, you can create it as a graphic with another program and import it into the program.

That represents a brief list of the important features of *Ventura Publisher*, including the organizational structure of its files. It's a little more complicated than a word processor, but you'll get the hang of it quickly.

This book covers version 2 of *Ventura Publisher*. Earlier versions 1 and 1.1 will probably conform to most of the explanations in this book. Some of the more salient improvements between versions are listed in Chapter 7.

Chapter 2
Introduction to
Ventura Publisher

Chapter 2
Introduction to
Ventura Publisher

Let's pause for a moment and take a look at what we're getting into. Figure 2-1 shows the *Ventura Publisher* main screen.

In Chapter 4, you'll see how to install the program and prepare the fonts for use, but let's take a momentary tour of the actual product. Treat this chapter as a sort of reference. If you can't find a feature, look here and your search will be a little easier.

If you're not entirely comfortable with a windowing environment, like GEM (the operating system that forms the basis for *Ventura Publisher)*, you should read through this chapter more carefully because it gives important information about GEM's operation. If you've heard that GEM (or any windowing environment) is user-friendly and simple to understand, you should be warned: Windowing environments like GEM and *Windows* are only a little more logical than command-line environments like MS-DOS and CP/M. *User-friendly* should be taken as a relative term.

But don't worry. You'll learn it quickly. It's this rapidness of learning that makes the window environment superior. If this is your first experience with GEM, don't feel foolish if you get lost or forget a technique. After you've worked through a few sessions with *Ventura Publisher*, GEM will be second nature to you.

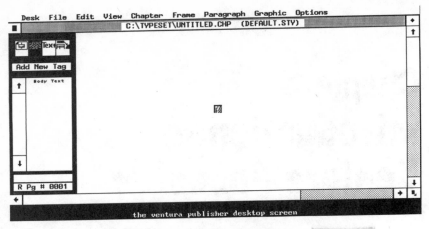

Figure 2-1. The *Ventura Publisher* Main Screen

The Menus

Across the top of the screen you can see the nine main menu items:

Desk
File
Edit
View
Chapter
Frame
Paragraph
Graphic
Options

Clicking on any of these will cause a menu to drop down. The menu names distinguish the items available on the menus fairly well, but the following pages will show each of the menus in turn, and list each of the items available on the menu. Note that several of these menus have items with three dots following their names. These three dots (known as an *ellipsis*) indicate that selecting the item will pull up a dialog box full of options. It would take too

14

many pages to show all the dialog boxes and explain the items on each in turn. Some of these dialog boxes will be shown in the chapters that lead you through the process of creating publications. By the time you finish with this book, you'll be able to make sense of the dialog boxes that aren't explicitly explained here.

You'll also note that some of the items are not as clearly visible as others. When an item is shaded (like *Cut Frame* in Figure 2-2), the specific item isn't available at this time. *Ventura Publisher* has four separate modes of operation:

- Frame
- Paragraph
- Text
- Graphic

All items on the menus aren't available at all times in all phases of the program. When you see an item you need to use and it's shaded, it's an indication that you need to change modes before accessing that option, or you may need to click on a paragraph or frame, or create a graphic image, before the item is available.

Because some of the items are a little difficult to read, the menu items will be listed along with the figure.

Some of the menus offer slightly different selections in the various phases of the program. For instance, *Cut Frame* in Figure 2-2 will change to *Cut Graphic* when you are working in graphic mode.

Keyboard shortcuts. Note that some of the menu items have additional text off to the right. A caret (^) means you should hold down Ctrl and then type the key indicated (like ^S in Figure 2-3: Hold down Ctrl and type *S* to save your work). The upward-pointing arrow (↑ as seen in Figure 2-2, next to Copy Frame) indicates that you should press the Shift key and type the indicated key, the Delete key in this case.

There are quite a few special keyboard shortcuts like these, and not all are indicated on the menus. See Appendix A for additional keyboard shortcuts.

15

Toggled items. Some menu items are like switches that can be turned off and on. Look at the item *Frame Setting* in Figure 2-4. The check mark beside this item indicates that it's turned on. That is, the program is currently in frame-setting mode. In the Options menu (Figure 2-9) all the options that begin with *Hide* change to *Show* when they are selected, and all the options that end with *Off* are toggled to *On* when selected.

Desk

This selection is a bit of vanity on the part of the programmers. Selecting it gives you one option: Publisher Info. . . . Choosing this option calls up a dialog box full of developers' names and gives some basic information about your version of *Ventura Publisher,* such as the serial number, version, and so on.

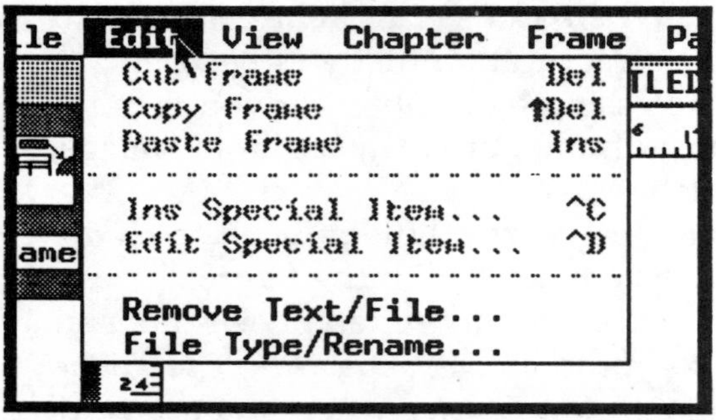

Figure 2-2. The Edit Menu

Edit

Cut Frame	Del
Copy Frame	↑Del (Shift-Del)
Paste Frame	Ins
Ins Special Item	^C
Edit Special Item	^D
Remove Text/File	
File Type/Rename	

Figure 2-3. The File Menu

File

New	
Open Chapter. . .	
Save	^S (Ctrl-S)
Save As. . .	
Abandon. . .	
Load Text/Picture. . .	
Load Diff. Style. . .	
Save As New Style. . .	
To Print. . .	
DOS File Ops. . .	
Quit	

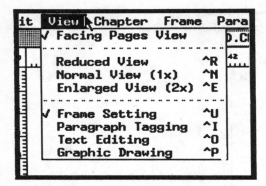

Figure 2-4. The View Menu

View

Facing Pages View	
Reduced View	^R
Normal View (1×)	^N
Enlarged View (2×)	^E
Frame Setting	^U
Paragraph Tagging	^I
Text Editing	^O
Graphic Drawing	^P

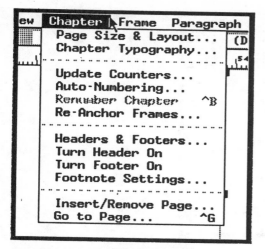

Figure 2-5. The Chapter Menu

Chapter

Page Size & Layout. . .
Chapter Typography. . .
Update Counters. . .
Auto-Numbering. . .
Renumber Chapter. . .   ^B
Re-Anchor Frames. . .
Headers & Footers. . .
Turn Header On
Turn Footer On
Footnote Settings. . .
Insert/Remove Page. . .
Go to Page. . .   ^G

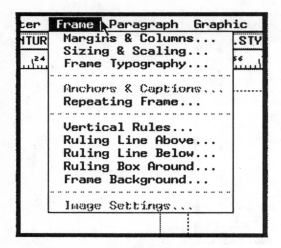

Figure 2-6. The Frame Menu

Frame

Margins & Columns. . .
Sizing & Scaling. . .
Frame Typography. . .
Anchors & Captions. . .
Repeating Frame. . .
Vertical Rules. . .
Ruling Line Above. . .
Ruling Line Below. . .
Ruling Box Around. . .
Frame Background. . .
Image Settings. . .

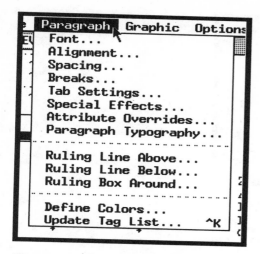

Figure 2-7. The Paragraph Menu

Paragraph

Font. . .
Alignment. . .
Spacing. . .
Breaks. . .
Tab Settings. . .
Special Effects. . .
Attribute Overrides. . .
Paragraph Typography. . .
Ruling Line Above. . .
Ruling Line Below. . .
Ruling Box Around. . .
Define Colors. . .
Update Tag List. . .   ^K

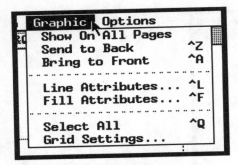

Figure 2-8. The Graphic Menu

Graphic

Show On All Pages
Send to Back   ^Z
Bring to Front   ^A
Line Attributes. . .   ^L
Fill Attributes. . .   ^F
Select All   ^Q
Grid Settings. . .

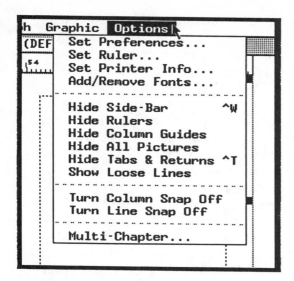

Figure 2-9. The Options Menu

Options

Set Preferences. . .
Set Ruler. . .
Set Printer Info. . .
Add/Remove Fonts. . .
Hide Side-Bar   ^W
Hide Rulers
Hide Column Guides
Hide All Pictures
Hides Tabs & Returns   ^T
Show Loose Lines
Turn Column Snap Off
Turn Line Snap Off
Multi-Chapter

Mouse Maneuvers

There are three kinds of mouse maneuvers that will concern you in this book: *clicking, double-clicking,* and *dragging.*

Clicking. Clicking is accomplished by moving the mouse pointer to a menu item and rapidly pressing and releasing the left mouse button (*Ventura Publisher* only uses the left mouse button).

If you are among the growing minority of people who have come to hate mice, you can emulate the mouse:

Press Ctrl-Right Shift. Your computer should beep to indicate it has changed to keyboard control. Press the cursor keys until your mouse pointer is pointing to the item you want to select and then tap the Home key. This action is even less comfortable than using the mouse. As computers move on into the next generation, you'll have to get used to mice. You might as well start now. However, if you don't own a mouse, or the computer you're using isn't set up for one, this is an alternate way of running the program.

When you're using this mouse emulation, you'll be unable to move the text cursor with the cursor keys, so switch out of mouse-emulation mode by pressing Ctrl-Right Shift again when you begin to edit text.

Double clicking. In dialog boxes, you can choose the option you want and exit the box by rapidly clicking the left mouse button twice on your selection. The keyboard alternative is to press Enter. A third alternative is to click once on the item you want to select and then click on the OK box.

Dragging. Dragging is accomplished by placing the mouse pointer on the item to be dragged, holding down the left mouse button, and then repositioning the mouse pointer. The item (or its ghost) will follow your pointer around the screen. When you release the button, the item will be deposited in the new location. The keyboard equivalent of dragging is accomplished as follows:

Press Ctrl-Right Shift and position the cursor with the cursor keys, then press the End key. You can then drag the item (such as the scroll box, described below) with the cursor keys. Press the Home key to release the item.

Once again, if you enter text mode and begin using the cursor keys to move the text cursor, you'll be surprised to see that the mouse pointer rather than the text cursor is affected. Turn off the keyboard mouse emulation. When you finish using the keyboard and you want to return to mouse mashing, press Ctrl-Right Shift again.

Fine control. Occasionally you won't want to use the gross movements of the mouse and the cursor keys. Positioning graphics on a pixel-by-pixel basis (*pixels* are the individual dots of phosphor on your monitor screen) is best accomplished with the keyboard cursor controls.

Press Ctrl-Right Shift. Your computer should beep to indicate it has changed to keyboard control. Then operate the cursor keys while holding down either Shift key. The mouse pointer and whatever it's dragging will move one pixel at a time in the direction of the arrow key.

For fine alignments, make sure Line and Column Snap are on in the Options menu (these will be explained later).

The GEM Screen

Ventura Publisher can be run under the GEM operating system. If you own and use that operating system, you probably need little further instruction. The program also has "run-time GEM" that operates just while the program is running. Most users will probably be operating under that system, and since GEM is a slightly unusual way of operating a computer, it will be covered briefly here. Digital Research (formerly known as Intergalactic Digital Research) would probably appreciate a mention at this point. They developed the GEM system to make the PC operate a little like a Macintosh. Some people swear by GEM. Others call it CP/M with windows (Digital Research invented the erstwhile operating system of choice, CP/M). You really have no choice but to use GEM with *Ventura Publisher;* however, if you *like* GEM, you can purchase the operating system and run a few selected applications under it, including some graphics programs.

There is much more to the *Ventura Publisher* screen than menus. Let's take a look at some of the GEM convenience items in turn. There are only a few and they're fairly intuitive, so you'll grasp them quickly when they're explained. Experiment with them to become familiar with their actions.

If you have used a Macintosh or a PC running *Windows,* GEM will be no mystery. If not, read on.

Scroll Bars

There are two scroll bars on the GEM screen. With them you can

- Edge the *Ventura Publisher* work screen to the left and right, or up and down. This screen is a window on the text, showing a limited part of the larger page underneath. You'll often want to reposition your view to see different parts of the page.
- Move proportionally through the current page.
- Move through the current page screen by screen.

Figure 2-10 shows the various parts of the scroll bars. Note that they're located at the right and bottom edges of the *Ventura Publisher* screen. Move your mouse pointer to an arrow and click. The screen will move slightly in the direction the arrow is pointing. Depending on what is on the screen at the time, you may move the distance of a line of type, or a couple of characters. This is the technique to use when you only want to move small distances.

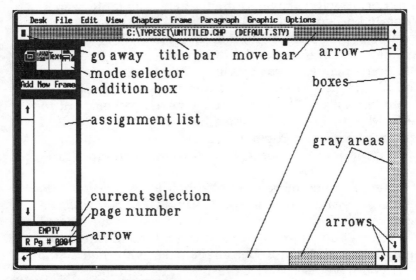

Figure 2-10. The GEM Screen

The boxes are used for moving proportionally through the page onscreen. You may notice that GEM scroll boxes are different from Macintosh and *Windows* scroll boxes because GEM boxes indicate by their sizes how much of the document is currently visible. If you want to move halfway across the page, place the mouse pointer on the scroll box at the bottom of the screen, press the left mouse button, and drag it about halfway through its travel. Then fine-tune by clicking on the arrows.

Finally, for gross adjustments, you can move a whole screen's width or height in any direction by clicking in the gray area between the arrow and the scroll box. You'll move in the direction of the arrow nearest the gray area you are clicking. This is a useful maneuver when working with an extremely expanded page.

Size Box, Go Away, Zoom Box, and Move Bar

In the lower right corner of Figure 2-10 you'll see the *size box*. You can drag the size box all around the screen. With it, you adjust the size of the current window. Why would you want to do that? You wouldn't. It's best to leave the size box alone.

In the upper left corner of the window is another box: the *go away* box. It's supposed to make the current window go away. It doesn't appear to work. Click it if you like. The window won't go away until you select *Quit* from the File menu.

The *zoom box* is in the upper right corner of the window. If you make the mistake of sizing your window, click this box to make it fill the screen again.

The *move bar* is used to reposition the window. If you want to see it in action, size the window smaller to make some space and then drag the window by its move bar (see "Mouse Maneuvers," above). You can move the window anywhere on the visible screen. Once again, why would you want to do that? If you were able to open multiple *Ventura Publisher* windows, you could use this feature to place them in better positions relative to each other, but you can only have one *Ventura Publisher* window open at a time. When

27

you finish moving the window, click on the zoom box and the window will return to its full-screen size and its correct position.

Perhaps in some future *Ventura Publisher* there will be a purpose for these controls. For now, consider them window dressing.

Title Bar

In the middle of the move bar is the title of the current document. Note that in the figure it indicates that an untitled chapter is loaded (UNTITLED.CHP), along with the default style (DEFAULT.STY).

Work Section

At the left side of the screen are the tools that allow you to work with your document.

Mode selector. At the top of this area is the mode selector. The four boxes in this area correspond to the four modes of *Ventura Publisher* operation: frame, paragraph, text, and graphic mode. If you perused the section on menus earlier in this chapter, these selections will sound familiar. In fact, clicking on one of these boxes is the same as selecting the mode from the View menu, but simpler and quicker.

Addition box. In various modes, you'll want to add tags or frames, or change the font. When you do, click on this box (or press Ctrl-2).

Assignment list. Note that this list has a tiny scroll bar. It's used when the list of options is longer than the window can accommodate. Briefly, if you want to have all the heads in a newsletter look the same (as you probably will), click on the paragraph box in the mode selector, and load a newsletter style with the option *Load Diff. Style* on the File menu. When the new style is loaded, all the options associated with that style will appear in the assignment list. For instance, some styles will include

- Body text
- Bullet
- Byline

28

- Creditline
- Deckhead
- Firstpar

You would select the paragraph you want to take on the style (by clicking on it with the paragraph cursor) and then click on the tag in the assignment list to assign the tag to the paragraph. It's all much simpler than it sounds. Don't worry about it right now. This will be fully covered later.

Current selection. If you assigned the Firstpar (first paragraph) tag to the selected paragraph on the example above, the current selection box would contain the text *Firstpar* whenever you select the paragraph again in paragraph mode. In frame mode, it contains the name of the file in the current frame.

Page number. This item, in addition to displaying the current page, will indicate whether the current page is a left or right page, and, when a long chapter is being reformatted, it will show what page is currently being updated.

The Text Screen

The most important part of the *Ventura Publisher* screen is the work area. This is the area where you'll do most of your work. There isn't much to say about this area until we actually get into laying out a document. You'll begin to use it in Chapter 5. You should at least scan the intervening material. Some points are discussed that could save you some time and heartache in using *Ventura Publisher*.

Equipment

What do you need to run *Ventura Publisher?* The bare minimum is a 640K PC or compatible with a hard disk and a dot-matrix printer. This will turn out perfectly acceptable results for family or friends, church groups, and others for whom the message is more important than the medium, and for whom time is not an issue. A PC is (generally speaking) quite slow, and even an XT clone is frustratingly slow, even when creating a small document. You'll often wish you had a faster computer. The difference a faster CPU like the 80286 or the 80386 will make is far greater than a simple comparison of clock speeds would lead you to believe.

Likewise, a dot-matrix printer will create a publication that looks perfectly acceptable—until you put it beside one that was created with a laser printer. And neither of these can hold a candle to the appearance of a typeset publication. If you have hundreds of dollars at your disposal, buy a dot-matrix printer. If you have thousands, buy a laser printer. And if you have tens of thousands or a budget large enough to cover the high leasing costs, turn to typesetting.

You don't really need a mouse to run the program, but once again, you'll find yourself wishing you had one. Mice are widely available for $100 or less (often this includes some high-quality graphics software), so there's no good excuse not to buy one.

The equipment you bring to the task can vary broadly. You'll probably want to have something better than the bare minimum.

All the figures and layouts in this book were created with a PC XT-compatible based on an 8088-2 CPU (about 8 MHz), with 640K and a 30MB hard drive, driving a Star LaserPrinter 8 with 2MB RAM. I was grateful for the loan of *ComputerEyes* by Digital Vision, a digitizing system with software for capturing composite (television or VCR) images, and *ScanMan*, the hand scanner from Logitech.

The PC I used is provided with a graphics card that can be switched between Hercules and CGA graphics. It was run in Hercules mode. There is little use for color in desktop publishing yet (and little use for the CGA in anything at all). Color laser printers are arriving, but they're outrageously expensive. And when you have something color-laser printed, how will you publish it? It would be prohibitively expensive to create hundreds of color-laser prints, or color photocopies. You would end up color separating the material anyway if you wanted more than a few dozen copies, and color-laser printing will only add another level of distortion and loss of resolution to the process. If you absolutely must have color, *Ventura Publisher* will do the separation for you (see Chapter 7). Take the separated images to a professional printer and be prepared to spend a large amount of money. As of now, color desktop publishing is in its early infancy.

The pages you print will probably be in black-and-white (purists believe any colors on the page besides black, white, and red are an abomination anyway), so there's no reason to spend hundreds of dollars on EGA or VGA capability. A Hercules card with a monochrome monitor will serve you better than a color card. Overall, it's a pleasant screen to look at, it provides a large number of pixels, and gives a fairly clear picture of what will eventually appear on the page.

To run *Ventura Publisher,* you'll need:

- IBM PC, XT, AT, PS/2, or compatible
- 640K RAM
- Hard disk with around 6MB of free space
- Graphics video board: Hercules, EGA, VGA, Genius, Wyse 700, AT & T 6300, Xerox 6065, IBM Color Card, or something similar
- Mouse: Microsoft serial or bus, PS/2 mouse, Mouse Systems mouse, or compatible
- MS-/PC-DOS 2.1 or a more recent version
- Printer: PostScript-compatible, Epson MX/RX/FX/LQ, Star, or other HP-compatible laser printer. These printers and their compatibles represent most available printers. If your printer isn't listed here, check the manual for an exhaustive list of supported printers.

Help

You may find yourself unable to proceed with your work because you have a question. In many cases the answer to your question is available right in the currently open dialog box. A tiny rectangle containing a question mark appears in the upper right corner of most dialog boxes. Click on this rectangle and you'll see a menu of help topics. When you click on the topic that most closely matches your question, you'll see a dialog box like the one in Figure 2-11.

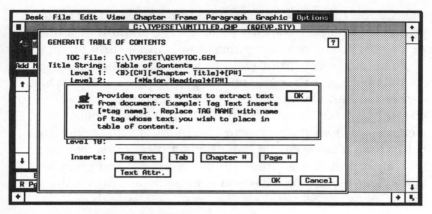

Figure 2-11. A Help Dialog Box

The next line of defense is the table of contents and index of this book. Use them to locate the answers you need. Most will be in one of those two places. If your question is of a more technical nature, refer to the user's manual that came with *Ventura Publisher*. It's thorough, but you may have some trouble with its organization.

Finally, if you are a registered user and you've been working with *Ventura Publisher* for 60 days or less, you can call the support number 1-214-436-2616. *Ventura Publisher* support people are well known for their expertise and patience. They were very helpful to me during the creation of this book. You can continue this support indefinitely at a cost of $150 per year. If you are a professional, this can be a bargain that saves you many lost man-hours. Finally, *Ventura Publisher* has a bulletin board that can be of some use. The number is 1-408-227-4818.

Chapter 3
Backups

Chapter 3
Backups

Everything you do on a computer is subject to loss. If you don't regularly save your work, you are at the mercy of the power lines. A momentary loss of power would wipe out everything in memory. Most people save their work periodically, but few realize how quickly the risk builds when they don't save their work often.

If you are a conservative person who saves your work once an hour, you run the risk of losing an hour's work in the event of a loss of power. For some people, this doesn't represent much of a loss, but others can generate a great deal of text in an hour's time. I prefer to save every five to ten minutes. Every day I save my currently active files on a floppy diskette. Once a week, I run a backup program that saves all my hard disk files on a seemingly infinite series of floppies.

But one thing that many otherwise conscientious people forget or neglect to do is back up their original application disks, particularly when the application is being installed on a hard disk. You still have to back up the application disks, even though you don't use them every day. Having a hard disk "go bad" isn't unusual. They're more fragile than diskettes in many ways. If or when you lose your hard disk for whatever reason, or if you accidentally delete all the files in one of your application directories, you'll want to be sure your application files are available in a safe place.

Another reason you'll want your back up application is for reinstalling files. Files on a hard disk have a funny way of getting overwritten at inopportune moments. You'll want to reinstall your application if you change printers or buy a better display card. You have to go through at least part of the installation process to upgrade *Ventura Publisher* to work with your new hardware. Since you'll be using your application disks periodically, you should do the installing from backup disks, not the originals.

Creating Backup Disks for the Application

This is a very simple procedure. With your copy of *Ventura Publisher* you received a number of floppy disks. The number of disks may vary over time as versions come and go, and as features are added. The disks may be 5¼-inch or 3½-inch diskettes. Buy a number of blank diskettes of the same size as the *Ventura Publisher* application disks. If there are 11 diskettes with your package, buy two 10-count boxes of disks for the backup. You'll certainly use the extra diskettes for something. I've never heard anyone complain about having too many floppy disks.

If You Have Two Similar Floppy Drives

If you have two 5¼-inch or two 3½-inch drives, put Disk #1 in the A: drive. Put your first backup disk in the B: drive. Type *DISKCOPY A: B:* and press Enter. It will take a few minutes for the copy to complete. If the backup diskette isn't formatted, the DISKCOPY command will take care of that for you. While the backup is in progress, pull out a disk label (if you bought bargain basement diskettes, you may not have labels. Use address labels, if necessary. You must label the backup diskettes). Write Disk #1 on the label. When the copy is completed, put disk #2 in drive A:, and your second backup diskette in drive B:. Your computer will ask if you want to copy another diskette. Type *Y* and respond to the next prompt by pressing Enter. Apply the first disk label to backup disk #1. Put your first two disks back in their sleeves and start writing a label for backup disk #2. Continue until all the disks are backed up. Put the original disks in some very safe place far from your computer, in another part of town, if possible. Only use the backup disks for installing or reinstalling *Ventura Publisher*.

If You Have One Floppy Drive or Your Drives Are Dissimilar

You can't do a DISKCOPY with dissimilar drives. If you have only one drive or dissimilar drives, insert Disk #1 in the A: drive and enter

DISKCOPY A: A:

You'll be prompted to insert the SOURCE diskette in drive A:. Press any key when you're ready. The disk drive will labor for a few seconds, and then prompt you to insert the TARGET diskette in drive A:. Place the backup disk in drive A: and press any key. While the backup is taking place, prepare a label for your backup disk that somehow indicates that it's a copy of Disk #1.

Continue the process until all the disks are backed up. Hide your originals in a safe location far from your backups and your computer, perhaps in a relative's house.

Only use your backup disks for installing or reinstalling *Ventura Publisher*.

Backing Up Your Work

All your files on the hard disk should also be backed up regularly. You can always contact Xerox if you lose all copies of the application (IF you are a registered user, that is—otherwise, you can always buy another copy of *Ventura Publisher*), but who is going to have a spare copy of your presentation, your helpful hamburger hints book, or your bowling league newsletter? Like the song says: *Only you.*

The way to back up is to keep all your personal files in a separate subdirectory on your hard disk. Then at the end of each day's work, copy them over to a floppy. When the floppy reaches its capacity, take a hard look at your files. Chances are that one or more files are rarely used. Place these files in a separate directory for archive files. Place them on yet another floppy disk, a disk you only need to update on the rare occasion that one or more of the archive files are changed.

Consider purchasing a backup utility like *PC Tools Deluxe* to make complete backups of your hard disk on a regular

basis. It takes a lot of the worry out of hard disk manage-
ment. If you're rich as Croesus, buy a tape backup. But
whatever your approach to the subject, back up regularly,
and consider keeping several backup copies: Rotate three or
four copies on a daily basis and do one heavy-duty backup
weekly or monthly, depending on the time you can devote
to backups and the value of your time and effort.

Chapter 4
Installation

Chapter 4
Installation

There are so many computers that will run *Ventura Publisher*, and so many printers, that it would be self-defeating to cover them all. Instead, I'll concentrate on a typical installation. The instructions that follow will apply to most computers, but the particular computer being used is an 8088 XT-compatible. It has a 30MB hard disk an two 360K floppy drives. It also has a mouse. You'll need a hard drive to use *Ventura Publisher*, as well as any other serious desktop publishing package. A mouse is a convenience item, but an important one.

PC compatibles and hard disks can be obtained at bargain prices virtually anywhere. The only advantage in having a more expensive machine is in its speed, or perhaps, if you bought it from a local dealer, there may be an advantage in support. Generally speaking, though, unless the software specifically calls for a high-octane central processing unit like the 80286 or 80386, you can accomplish as much with a bargain-basement machine as with the hottest thing on the block. You'll just have to wait a bit longer for results.

The machine is hooked up to an HP-compatible laser printer (a Star LaserPrinter 8 with 2MB installed memory). Short of a very expensive typesetting machine, the best printer to use with *Ventura Publisher* is a laser printer, whether it supports PCL or PostScript. But again, you can achieve perfectly acceptable results for most applications with a 9- or 24-pin dot-matrix printer.

Installing *Ventura Publisher*

You'll note that there are two sets of disks that come with the *Ventura Publisher* package. One set of disks contains Bitstream Fontware, the software that allows you to produce high-quality printouts almost as clear as typeset text. That software will be discussed later in the chapter. The other set of disks concerns us right now.

Begin installing *Ventura Publisher* with Disk #1. Put it in your A: drive and enter

A:VPPREP

You'll see the screen shown in Figure 4-1.

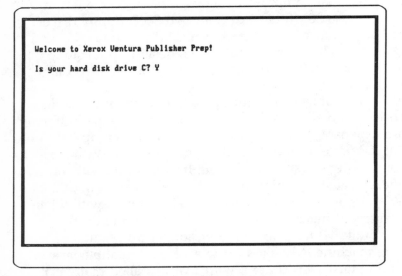

Welcome to Xerox Ventura Publisher Prep!

Is your hard disk drive C? Y

Figure 4-1. Beginning Installation Screen

A series of screens will appear, each asking for a piece of information. The opening screen confirms that your hard disk is drive C:. Hit return if it is C:, or type in the correct drive letter.

The next screen asks if you're installing this version of *Ventura Publisher* for the first time. Press Enter if this is the first time, or type *N* and press Enter if you've installed the software on this machine on a previous occasion. If you're upgrading from version 1.1, simply reinstall the program.

If you're upgrading from version 1.0, you'll have to delete all the files in your GEM directories:

\GEMSYS
\GEMBOOT
\GEMDESK
\GEMAPPS
\GEMAPPS\VPSYS

And you'll have to remove these directories. You won't need them for the new version of *Ventura Publisher*.

The next screen informs you that the files are being copied to your hard disk. It takes perhaps a minute to install. Then you'll be prompted to remove Disk #1 and insert Disk #2. Do so, and press Enter to continue. You'll be prompted to change disks several times as all the files are copied to your hard disk.

You'll be asked whether to install the example files. If you have large amounts of hard disk space, press Enter to install the example files. You can always remove them later, but for the moment, while learning this software, you'll benefit from having them on disk. Press Enter when asked whether to install the tutorials. This will take a few minutes.

You'll be prompted to change disks again. Disk #5 is a setup disk. So far, installation has been a no-brainer. Now you're going to have to demonstrate some knowledge of your system. The first question is, *Which graphics card and display do you have?* (See Figure 4-2.)

Simply type the letter that corresponds to your graphics display. I'm running the program with a Hercules-compatible card, so I typed *G*.

The next screen will ask you what sort of mouse you have (Figure 4-3).

Press the letter that corresponds to your mouse.

The next screen asks you what sort of printer you're using (Figure 4-4).

```
Which graphics card and display do you have?

A   IBM CGA or compatible / Color Display (640x200).
B   IBM EGA or compatible / Color Display (640x200) 2 colors.
C   IBM EGA or compatible / Enhanced Display (640x350) 2 colors.
D   IBM EGA or compatible / Monochrome PC Display (640x350).
E   IBM VGA or compatible (640x480) 2 colors.
F   IBM PS/2 Model 30 MCGA or compatible (640x480).
G   Hercules Card or compatible / Monochrome PC Display (720x348).
H   Xerox 6065 / AT&T 6300 (640x400).
I   MDS Genius Full Page Display (720 x 1000).
J   Xerox Full Page Display (720 x 992).
K   Wyse WY-700 Display (1280 x 800).
L   THESE DRIVERS SHOULD BE USED FOR COLOR OR GREY SCALE (EMS RECOMENDED)
M   IBM EGA or compatible / Color Display (640x200) 16 colors.
N   IBM EGA or compatible / Enhanced Display (640x350) 16 colors.

Press PgDn for additional options or
Type the letter of the graphics card you have:
```

Figure 4-2. Graphics Setup

```
Which mouse do you have?

A   No Mouse
B   PC Mouse or Mouse Systems Compatible / SummaMouse
C   Xerox, AT&T, Microsoft Buss Mouse ( Uses MOUSE.COM )
D   Microsoft Serial Mouse ( RS232 )
E   IBM PS/2 Mouse
F   SummaSketch 1201 with Stylus
G   SummaSketch 1201 with Cursor
H   SummaSketch 961  with Stylus
I   SummaSketch 961  with Cursor
J   SummaSketch 1812 with Stylus
K   SummaSketch 1812 with Cursor

Type the letter of the mouse you have:
```

Figure 4-3. Mouse Setup

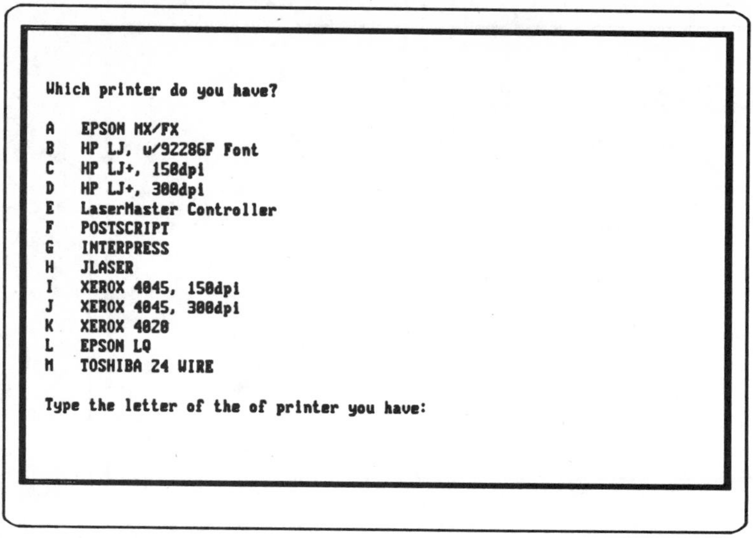

```
Which printer do you have?

A    EPSON MX/FX
B    HP LJ, w/92286F Font
C    HP LJ+, 150dpi
D    HP LJ+, 300dpi
E    LaserMaster Controller
F    POSTSCRIPT
G    INTERPRESS
H    JLASER
I    XEROX 4045, 150dpi
J    XEROX 4045, 300dpi
K    XEROX 4020
L    EPSON LQ
M    TOSHIBA 24 WIRE

Type the letter of the of printer you have:
```

Figure 4-4. Printer Setup

Press the letter that corresponds to your printer. You'll be asked to which port your printer is attached (Figure 4-5).

Then a screen will appear asking whether you want to add another printer. If you have more than one printer, type Y and press Enter and you'll be led through the printer installation screens shown in Figures 4-4 and 4-5 again. Many people will *proof* their work on a dot-matrix printer and then print the final version on a laser printer.

Xerox recommends that if you have an HP Laserjet Plus (or compatible) capable of both 150 and 300 dpi (dots per inch) printing, you should install drivers for each of these print densities. Sometimes when printing, the HP runs out of RAM and can't continue printing at 300 dpi. In that situation, you can simply switch to 150 dpi printing and continue with some loss of resolution.

When you've installed all of your printers, exit this loop by simply pressing Enter when you're asked whether to add additional printers.

Depending on the graphics card you selected earlier,

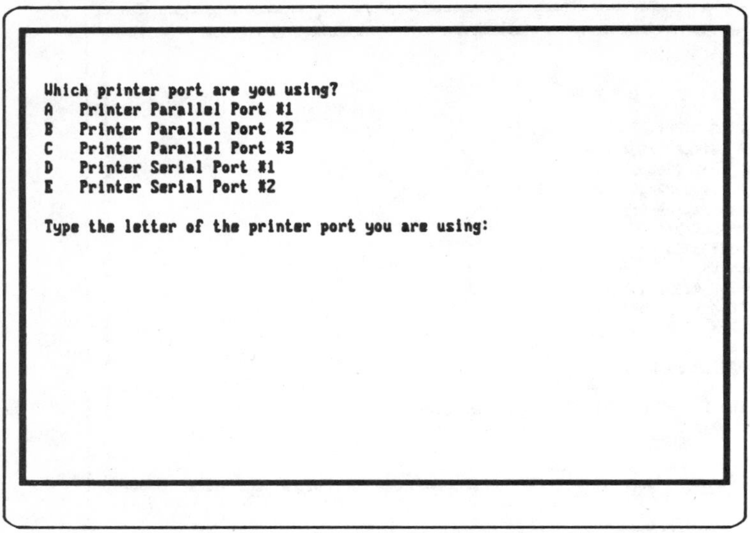

```
Which printer port are you using?
A    Printer Parallel Port #1
B    Printer Parallel Port #2
C    Printer Parallel Port #3
D    Printer Serial Port #1
E    Printer Serial Port #2

Type the letter of the printer port you are using:
```

Figure 4-5. Printer Port Setup

you'll be instructed to place a specific disk (Disk #6 or #7) in the drive and press Enter. Then you'll be told to insert the Screen Fonts disk (Disk #8). This will install the fonts you'll see onscreen. Getting those fonts to your printer is a more complicated business. It will be covered shortly. Finally you'll be prompted to place a printer driver disk in the drive (either Disk #9 or #10).

Again, depending on the printer you selected, you'll be told to insert a printer fonts disk. Some printers require more than one disk. If you selected more than one printer, you'll be prompted to insert additional disks in turn.

These font files are severely compressed and will have to be "unpacked" before they can be used. The installation program will take care of that for you. But you should be aware that it will take several minutes. Take a coffee break. When you return, we'll install the Bitstream Fontware.

Installing Bitstream Fontware

Before you begin installing printer fonts, be aware that their installation can literally take hours of computer time. (To

46

save some time, you might want to look at an alternate source of fonts mentioned in Appendix F: VS Software's *FontPaks*.) Once you select the fonts you need and start the computer on its task of creating the fonts, you'll be informed of the length of time it will require. You may be shocked. If you're conservative about your need for fonts, you might only have to wait an hour or two for their creation. If you're generous with fonts, you might as well set it up to run overnight. Bear in mind also that the fonts (particularly the larger versions) can take up enormous amounts of hard disk space. If you only have a few megabytes, you'll either have to compromise on the number of fonts you use or sacrifice some of your less important software and text and data files.

You need to make fonts for screen display and for your printer. Fontware allows you to produce output with a typeset look on a laser printer, or a highly attractive appearance (not quite typeset quality) on a dot-matrix printer.

Find the disk marked *Fontware Installation Kit*. Insert it into drive A: and type on the command line

A:FONTWARE

This is the name of a batch file on the floppy disk that starts up the installation program. After a few seconds you'll see the opening screen (Figure 4-6).

If you see colors on the screen (a sneaky way to determine whether you're using a color graphics card and monitor) type *Y* and press Enter; if not, type *N* and press Enter.

After you make your selection, you'll move on to the menu screen shown in Figure 4-7. You want to set up Fontware at this point, so use the cursor keys to make sure this selection is highlighted, and press Enter.

You'll see the directory setup screen (Figure 4-8).

The program will then copy many files to your hard disk. *Ventura Publisher* alone takes up about 3MB. The amount of disk space used by the fontware is essentially limitless. Unless your hard disk is huge or virtually empty, you'll probably end up making some sacrifices for your fonts.

After your disk drive has run for a few minutes, you'll

47

Figure 4-6. Fontware Opening Screen

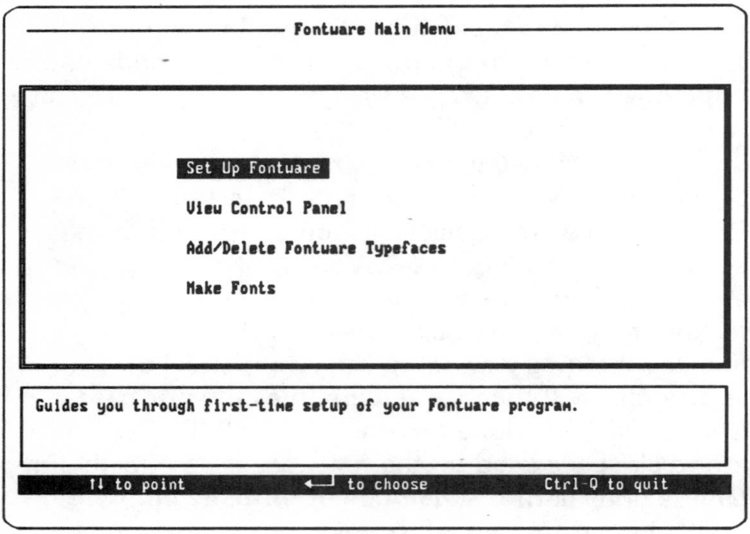

Figure 4-7. Fontware Main Menu

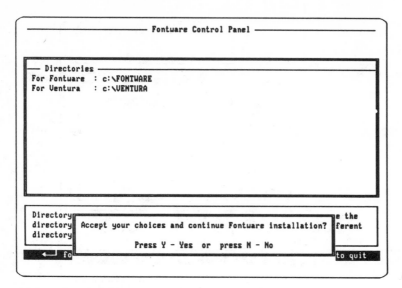

Figure 4-8. Directory Setup

be prompted to trade to the next disk. You should be pretty good at trading disks by now. While that disk is unpacking, there's time to tell you that the remaining Fontware disks contain font *families*. One is Dutch, which is a font very similar to Times-Roman, a handsome body font that will look good in the main text of books, pamphlets, and newsletters. Another is Swiss, which is a sans serif font good for headings but not much use for body text. The most common mistake of a beginning desktop publisher is to use a sans serif font in the main body of a text. It will look beautiful onscreen, but on paper, it's virtually impossible to read for very long. If you must use it in the body text, try to use narrow columns and lots of space between lines.

The last disk contains symbols and a proportional font with serifs a little like a typewriter font. This has its uses, but don't make the mistake of using it for long stretches. Stick to Dutch for that.

After the second disk has unloaded a few files, it will pause to ask what sort of display you have. Use the cursor keys to highlight the display and press Enter (Figure 4-9).

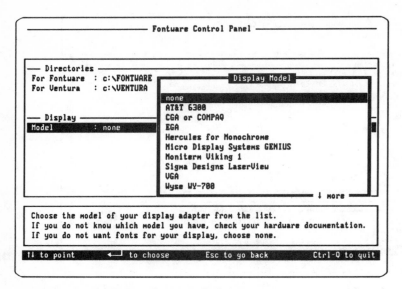

```
─────────────────── Fontware Control Panel ───────────────────

  ── Directories ──────────────────────────────────────────
  For Fontware  : c:\FONTWARE ┌──────── Display Model ────────┐
  For Ventura   : c:\VENTURA   │ none                          │
                               │ AT&T 6300                     │
  ── Display ──────────────    │ CGA or COMPAQ                 │
  Model         : none         │ EGA                           │
                               │ Hercules for Monochrome       │
                               │ Micro Display Systems GENIUS  │
                               │ Moniterm Viking 1             │
                               │ Sigma Designs LaserView       │
                               │ VGA                           │
                               │ Wyse WY-700                   │
                               └──────────────────  ↓ more ────┘

  ── Choose the model of your display adapter from the list.
     If you do not know which model you have, check your hardware documentation.
     If you do not want fonts for your display, choose none.

  ↑↓ to point      ← to choose      Esc to go back      Ctrl-Q to quit
```

Figure 4-9. Graphics Display Selection

```
─────────────────── Fontware Control Panel ───────────────────

  ── Directories ──────────────────────────────────────────
  For Fontware  : c:\FONTWARE ┌──── Display Character Set ────┐
  For Ventura   : c:\VENTURA   │                               │
                               │ VP US                         │
                               │ PostScript Outline            │
  ── Display ──────────────    │ VP International               │
  Model         : Hercules for │ VP Symbol - non-PostScript    │
  Character Set : VP Internati └───────────────────────────────┘




  ── The VP International character set has 190 characters.
     Use this set for most Ventura Publisher applications.

  ↑↓ to point      ← to choose      Esc to go back      Ctrl-Q to quit
```

Figure 4-10. Character Set Selection

50

Then you'll be prompted to enter the character set you want to use. VP US is a limited character set most useful in creating large headlines. If you want an emphasis on nonalphanumeric symbols for use in mathematical or engineering texts, select *VP Symbol*. For most users of *Ventura Publisher*, the best option is the default. Press Enter to select *VP International*. Don't select PostScript Outline. It has nothing to do with your screen display.

Once again you'll be asked what kind of printer you'll be using. This time you'll only be given one choice. You can't set up to run more than one printer (Figure 4-11).

And finally, you'll be asked to select a character set to use with the printer. This time PostScript Outline is an option. Choose it if you have a PostScript printer. Once again, most users will be best served by the default, VP International. A few specialized users will prefer to use VP US or VP Symbol. You'll have to confirm the installation. If all is well (Figure 4-12), press F10. If you want to make changes, press Esc and you'll be taken through the menus again.

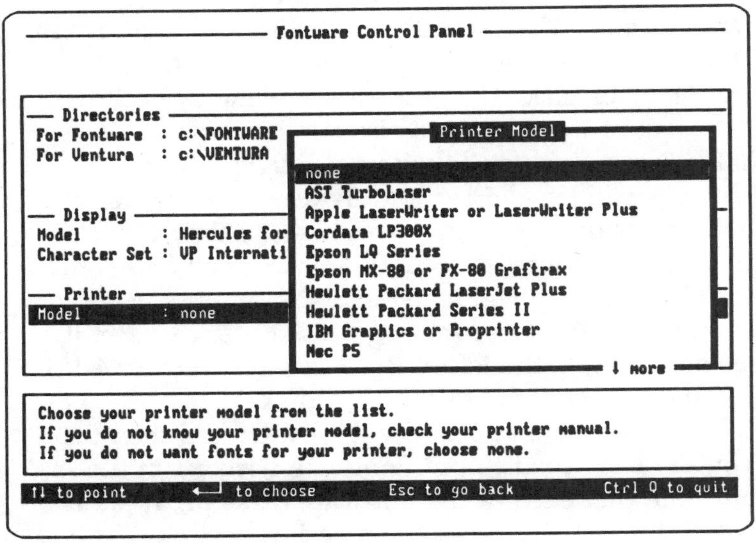

Figure 4-11. Printer Setup

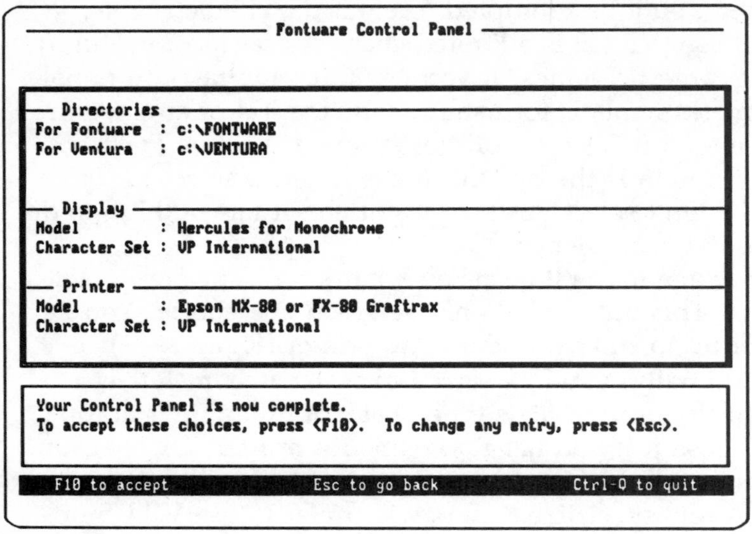

```
──────────────────── Fontware Control Panel ────────────────────

   ┌─ Directories ──────────────────────────────────────────────
   │ For Fontware  : c:\FONTWARE
   │ For Ventura   : c:\VENTURA
   │
   │
   ┌─ Display ──────────────────────────────────────────────────
   │ Model         : Hercules for Monochrome
   │ Character Set : VP International
   ┌─ Printer ──────────────────────────────────────────────────
   │ Model         : Epson MX-80 or FX-80 Graftrax
   │ Character Set : VP International


   Your Control Panel is now complete.
   To accept these choices, press <F10>.  To change any entry, press <Esc>.

  │ F10 to accept          Esc to go back          Ctrl-Q to quit │
```

Figure 4-12. Setup Confirmation Screen

Finally, you arrive at the typefaces screen. Currently there are no typefaces available (Figure 4-13).

As the prompt informs you at the bottom of Figure 4-13, press F3 to add fonts. You'll be prompted to put the Fontware Typeface disk #1 in the A: drive and press Enter. This is the disk containing the Swiss family of fonts: Swiss, Swiss Italic, Swiss Bold, and Swiss Bold Italic. These fonts are good for headlines and section dividers. You'll often use larger point sizes of these fonts, so when the time comes, consider making a limited selection of sizes in all four fonts. You'll see the screen in Figure 4-14.

As you highlight each font and press Enter to select it, you'll see an arrow to the left of the Swiss box (Figure 4-15). Press F10 to copy the fonts to the hard disk.

Similar screens will appear for the Dutch and the other fonts. You are prompted to put Fontware Disk #1 in the A: drive, but note that each of the fontware disks provided is marked *Disk 1 of 1*. Select your fonts and press Enter. The fonts provided represent the bare minimum you'll want for

52

```
┌──────────────── Fontuare Typefaces ────────────────────┐
│  ┌─ 0 Typefaces Available ──────────────────────────┐  │
│  │                                                   │  │
│  │                                                   │  │
│  │                                                   │  │
│  │                                                   │  │
│  │                                                   │  │
│  │                                                   │  │
│  │                                                   │  │
│  │                                                   │  │
│  └───────────────────────────────────────────────────┘  │
│  ┌───────────────────────────────────────────────────┐  │
│  │ Before you can make fonts, you must add typefaces to your system. │
│  │ To add a new typeface, press <F3>.                │  │
│  │ To return to the Main Menu, press <F10>.          │  │
│  └───────────────────────────────────────────────────┘  │
│  ███████████████████ Esc to Main Menu ████ Ctrl Q to quit ███│
│    F3 to add        F5 to delete         F10 to next menu │
└──────────────────────────────────────────────────────────┘
```

Figure 4-13. Typeface Screen

```
┌──────────────── Fontuare Typefaces ────────────────────┐
│  ┌─ 0 Typefaces Available ──────────────────────────┐  │
│  │                    ┌──── Typefaces ────────┐      │  │
│  │                    │ Swiss      Roman       │      │  │
│  │                    │            Italic      │      │  │
│  │                    │            Bold        │      │  │
│  │                    │            Bold Italic │      │  │
│  │                    └────────────────────────┘      │  │
│  │                                                   │  │
│  └───────────────────────────────────────────────────┘  │
│  ┌───────────────────────────────────────────────────┐  │
│  │ Point to each typeface you want to add and press <Enter>. │
│  │ An arrow appears next to each typeface you choose.│  │
│  │ After you have made your choices, press <F10> to copy. │
│  └───────────────────────────────────────────────────┘  │
│  ██████████████████ Esc to go back ████████ Ctrl Q to quit ██│
│    ↑↓  to point                            F10 to copy    │
│    ↵   to choose                                          │
└──────────────────────────────────────────────────────────┘
```

Figure 4-14. Swiss Typeface Screen

53

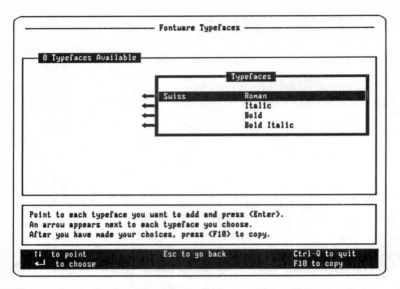

Figure 4-15. Swiss Typeface Screen with All Fonts Selected

desktop publishing with *Ventura Publisher*. After you work
with the software and become more seriously involved with
desktop publishing, you'll probably want to invest in more
fonts. You may also want to find a larger hard disk to accommodate them. When you have all the fonts uploaded to
your hard drive, it's time to tell the software to Make Fonts.
The fonts you've uploaded are only instructions to create the
actual fonts. Press F10. You'll see the screen shown in Figure
4-16.

As the instructions tell you, highlight the font you want
to create and press Enter. You'll be prompted for the point
sizes you require. For now, create 14- and 20-point Swiss in
all styles, 12-point Dutch in all styles, and 12-point Symbol A
Prop Serif. Figure 4-17 shows the screen with all point sizes
entered. Note that only a space separates the point sizes.
This may seem like a restricted number of fonts, and it is.
Bitstream recommends that you make roman-style (nonitalic)
fonts 6, 7, 8, 9, 10, 11, 12, 14, 16, 18, 20, 24, 28, and 36
points, but this takes staggering amounts of disk space and
takes many hours. Just for fun, specify all these sizes for all

54

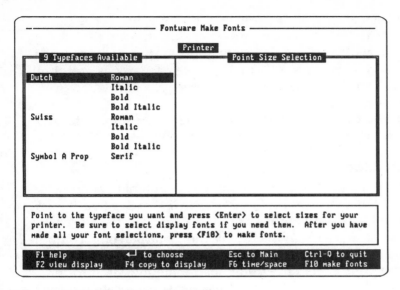

Figure 4-16. The Make Fonts Screen

```
┌─────────────────── Fontware Make Fonts ───────────────────┐
│                         ┌─────────┐                        │
│                         │ Printer │                        │
│   ┌ 9 Typefaces Available ┐     ┌ Point Size Selection ┐  │
│   │ Dutch         Roman   │     │                       │  │
│   │               Italic  │     │                       │  │
│   │               Bold    │     │                       │  │
│   │               Bold Italic │ │                       │  │
│   │ Suiss         Roman   │     │                       │  │
│   │               Italic  │     │                       │  │
│   │               Bold    │     │                       │  │
│   │               Bold Italic │ │                       │  │
│   │ Symbol A Prop Serif   │     │                       │  │
│   │                       │     │                       │  │
│   └───────────────────────┘     └───────────────────────┘  │
│   ┌─────────────────────────────────────────────────────┐  │
│   │ Point to the typeface you want and press <Enter> to select sizes for your │
│   │ printer.  Be sure to select display fonts if you need them.  After you have │
│   │ made all your font selections, press <F10> to make fonts. │
│   └─────────────────────────────────────────────────────┘  │
│   F1 help            ◄┘ to choose      Esc to Main    Ctrl-Q to quit │
│   F2 view display    F4 copy to display  F6 time/space  F10 make fonts │
└────────────────────────────────────────────────────────────┘
```

```
┌─────────────────── Fontware Make Fonts ───────────────────┐
│                         ┌─────────┐                        │
│                         │ Printer │                        │
│   ┌ 9 Typefaces Available ┐     ┌ Point Size Selection ┐  │
│   │ Dutch         Roman   │     │ 14 20                 │  │
│   │               Italic  │     │ 14 20                 │  │
│   │               Bold    │     │ 14 20                 │  │
│   │               Bold Italic │ │ 14 20                 │  │
│   │ Suiss         Roman   │     │ 12                    │  │
│   │               Italic  │     │ 12                    │  │
│   │               Bold    │     │ 12                    │  │
│   │               Bold Italic │ │ 12                    │  │
│   │ Symbol A Prop Serif   │     │ 12                    │  │
│   │                       │     │                       │  │
│   └───────────────────────┘     └───────────────────────┘  │
│   ┌─────────────────────────┐ ┌───────────────────────────┐ │
│   │ Ventura Style  : Normal │ │ Enter each size you want, followed by a │
│   │ Recommended Size: 6 and up │ │ a space.  Enter only whole numbers. │
│   │ Recommended Use : Text  │ │ Example: 9 18 24          │ │
│   └─────────────────────────┘ └───────────────────────────┘ │
│      ◄┘ to accept sizes     Esc to go back      Ctrl-Q to quit │
│      F1 help                                    F9 paste │
└────────────────────────────────────────────────────────────┘
```

Figure 4-17. The Make Fonts Screen with Point Sizes Entered

the available fonts and press F6 for a time and space estimate. Mine was 63 hours and more than the 10MB disk
space available. It's fairly easy to add fonts when you need
them and as you need them, so make as many as you think
you'll need. You can make more later (this is covered in
Chapter 6).

Press F10 to create the fonts. The time estimate for our
humble type box is one hour and 46 minutes.

Conclusion

That's all there is to installation. The chapters to come will
cover the use of *Ventura Publisher*. Now that *Ventura Publisher*
and the Bitstream Fontware are installed, you have no need
for the disks, right? Wrong. Few things in personal computing are so error-prone as a hard disk. Odds are that at some
point in your experience you'll lose something to error or
accident. Put your installation disks at some location far from
your hard disk and far from your original disks. That way no
disaster short of nuclear war is likely to destroy all the disks
at once. It wouldn't be far-fetched to put one set in a safe
deposit box, if you already have one. And ask an in-law with
whom you are on speaking terms to keep the other set. Or
keep a copy at work and one at home. Just make sure
they're all in safe places, which means they should be cool,
in the dark, and far from dirt, grease, and electromagnetism.

Chapter 5
Getting Started

Chapter 5
Getting Started

You'll never mistake *Ventura Publisher* for a word proccessor. It lacks virtually every feature that makes a word processor convenient and useful. Its main purpose is to exercise its considerable formatting power as it merges text and graphics from various files. (Its secondary purpose is to make you a member of an elite group. When you understand *Ventura Publisher*'s complex mass of formatting features, you'll belong to such an exclusive group, you'll practically be unique.)

Many people aren't crazy about the PC in general or GEM (the operating system under which *Ventura Publisher* runs) in particular. Others gush over the remarkable simplicity of *Ventura Publisher* and the inherent superiority of GEM. Try to adopt the attitude that they're neither plagues on humanity nor the promised land. They're tools. A tool is only as good as the amount of leverage it brings to the job.

Thinking About Publishing

When most people come to publishing, they have no concept of its complexity. Most come to it from word processing. In word processing, you have one principal concern: a single column of text on a single page. Sometimes you might write more than a single page, but a 20-page story on paper is simply a collection of 20 single pages as far as a word processor is concerned.

In publishing, you must think, first of all, in terms of facing pages (known as a *spread*). Your product will have print on the *recto* and the *verso*—the right and left sides (verso is the left page when you're looking at an open book—what you might normally think of as the back of the paper).

The two pages must fit together with harmony and balance—but not too much balance. There has to be some sense of energy in the layout, so the pages can't simply be mirror images of each other. We'll talk more about that later. Suffice it to say that when you open a book or magazine, you see two pages at once and they have to work as a team to convey the information needed and to attract and motivate the reader.

The second frame of reference in publishing is the work as a whole. You have to make decisions that affect the entire work. First of all, decide what the typeface will be. In this case, the Xerox people have helped out by providing a bare minimum of fonts. You can go out and spend many hundreds of dollars on Bitstream fonts, but choose carefully. You'll be hard pressed to find two fonts more attractive and more suited to their purpose than Dutch and Swiss. (These were the fonts provided with my copy; the fonts provided with your copy of *Ventura Publisher* may be different.)

Choose a dignified serif typeface like Dutch or Times-Roman for the body type and an attractive sans serif like Swiss or Helvetica for your heads. It's the style used in this book and many others. When you begin desktop publishing, you'll avoid many of the pitfalls if you find a professionally created book (or other publication) with an appearance that appeals to you and is similar to the publication you would like to create. When you find a publication that closely matches your taste, emulate it. An even better approach is to use (and modify as necessary) one of the stylesheets that came with *Ventura Publisher*. You can't go far off the track if you stick to the basics.

Be conservative at first. When you've published a few things, you'll be in a much better position to experiment.

If you decide to kick over the traces and opt for a sans serif body type, be my guest. You'll find many attractive magazines and books laid out this way. But make sure you leave a lot of white space between the lines (called *leading*—rhymes with breading) or your readers will be unable to read your publication for more than a paragraph or two. If you go completely beyond the pale and begin putting Chancery or

Old English in the body text, no one will be able to read it at all and you'll utterly defeat the purpose of publishing.

Go for It

Those carping asides out of the way, let's dive into the program. You should have some text to work with. Fortunately, Xerox has provided several training texts. Speaking from experience, though, it's more fun working with something you wrote yourself, or a project for school or work.

Load up and run *Ventura Publisher*. When you installed the program, it created a batch file in your root directory called VP.BAT that sets all the necessary switches and runs the program, so all you have to do to start the program is type *VP*. If you have anything running in the background, you'll probably have to get rid of it. *Ventura Publisher* is a ravenous memory hog. It wants all your memory. If you are able to add more than the base 640K memory to your machine, it would like that, too.

Here are the basic steps for beginning a publication (for convenience, they are abstracted in Appendix E).

Selecting a Stylesheet

For the purposes of this demonstration, we'll put together a newsletter. Most of the same principles apply to creating a book or other published piece, but a newsletter is a little more complicated because it involves more than one text. Our newsletter will be composed of three main articles and a graphic. But before we begin, you must select a stylesheet.

If you read the *New York Times*, *COMPUTE!*, or the *Saturday Review*, you'll probably have no trouble telling which you are reading at a given time. Open each of the magazines and you instantly know, without a glance at the cover, that the magazine in your hand is unique. What are some of the things that make the magazines and books you read so singular?

Typefaces and indents, decisions about spelling conventions, placement of advertisements, number of columns, leading, use of drop caps at the beginning of the lead paragraph, width of margins and gutters, floaters—these are just a few of the things that make up the soul of a publication, and they all involve *style*.

When *Ventura Publisher* is finally loaded, you'll have an untitled file in memory and the default stylesheet (see the top of the screen, just below the main menu). Pull down the File menu and select *Load Diff. Style. . . .* This will call up the Item Selector dialog box with all the available stylesheets listed in a window. Use the scroll bar to scroll until &NEWS-P3.STY appears. Double click on this selection and it will be loaded. This provides you with a three-column newsletter, which is what we'll create in this exercise.

When the stylesheet is completely loaded, pull down the File menu again and select *Save As New Style. . . .* Once again, you'll see the Item Selector dialog. Type in the name you want to give your stylesheet. The newsletter is going to be called *The Manchurian Candidate,* so for the examples used here, the stylesheet will be called MANCH.STY. Click on OK and the style will be saved. Your current style will also be changed to MANCH.STY.

Does that seem like an awful lot of rigamarole just to get started? Perhaps so, but it keeps the basic styles intact for later use. When people discover how talented you are at putting together newsletters, you may find yourself creating a dozen newsletters, and the style of each might be a small variation of the &NEWS-P3.STY stylesheet.

You could save some time and effort simply by copying and renaming the appropriate stylesheet file from DOS before loading up and running *Ventura Publisher*.

Creating a Chapter

Next, you must create your chapter. Pull down the File menu and select *Save As. . . .* In the resulting dialog box, enter the name of your chapter. You don't have to enter the file extension—*Ventura Publisher* will add the CHP extension for you. Save your chapter often (each time you make major changes or add a new file), using the *Save* command on the File menu. A chapter is simply a list of the files—text and graphics files, stylesheet, and others. Rather than repeatedly loading the text and graphic files that make up the newsletter, you'll assign them to a chapter, which will remember the names of the files and hold them ready for you as you create your newsletter. Whenever you start to work on *The Manchurian Candidate*, you need only load the chapter file (MANCH.CHP) to load all the text and graphic files that make up the document. You won't run out of space very quickly: You can have 128 files in a chapter.

Let's load the files that make up the newsletter. Pull down the File menu and click on *Load Text/Picture. . .* , which will call up the Load Text/Picture dialog (Figure 5-1).

At the top of this dialog box, you'll note the three items: Text, Line-Art, and Image. Later we'll load a graphic, but for now, leave Text selected. Choose the word processor whose files you are going to load (if your word processor isn't listed, you should save your files as ASCII for use with *Ventura Publisher*). The files all begin with MANCH.TXT (MANCH1.TXT, and so on). They're in *XyWrite* format, so click on that button and then the button that says *Several*, which allows you to import more than one text. And finally, click on OK to call up the next dialog box (Figure 5-2).

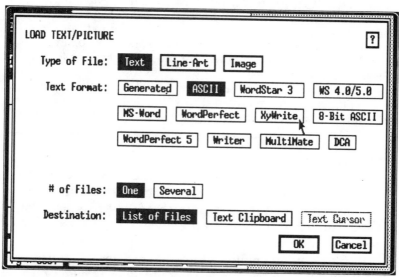

Figure 5-1. The Load Text/Picture Dialog

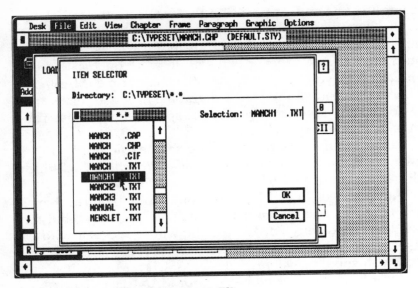

Figure 5-2. Calling Up the Text File

Ventura Publisher supports the following word processors and formats: DCA, Microsoft *Word*, *MultiMate*, *WordPerfect*, *WordStar*, *Xerox Writer*, and *XyWrite*. If you don't have one of these word processors, save your file in DCA format, a format compatible with one of these word processors, or in plain ASCII. Most word processors feature the ability to save to one of these formats.

Place a copy of the text file in the TYPESET subdirectory (the installation program added it to your root directory) to be used with *Ventura Publisher*.

Since *Several* was selected in the previous dialog box, double click on each file that belongs in the newsletter. Each time you double click, the file will be hyphenated and added to the assignment list. When you finish adding files, click on Cancel and you'll be returned to the document. There are some prepared files you could load, if you prefer, or you could load files you've created yourself—articles or short stories, for instance. *A word of warning: Only work on a COPY of the material you want to format. Ventura Publisher* pulls in the specific text you tell it to work on, alters it, and saves it back to disk in its altered state under its original filename. If you intend to work on an original text, copy it into the TYPESET directory *Ventura Publisher*'s installation program created on your hard disk. *Ventura Publisher* will look for it there and make all alterations on that copy of the file.

Now you should save your chapter. Select *Save* on the File menu. If your chapter is unnamed, you'll be prompted for a filename. You don't have to provide an extension. *Ventura Publisher* knows it's saving a chapter, and it will add the CHP extension automatically. If you leave *Ventura Publisher* and then return, pull down the File menu and select *Open Chapter.* . . . You'll see a dialog box with a directory and a slide bar. Manipulate the slide bar to bring your chapter into view. Double click on your chapter and it will load all the files that make up the chapter. This represents a terrific convenience. Imagine having to load up to 128 files individually from the Item Selector.

Page Size and Layout

Pull down the Chapter menu and select *Page Size & Layout* (Figure 5-3). It's possible (and probable) that the default settings in this box are acceptable to you (the alternatives are described in parentheses).

- *Orientation: Portrait.* Prints horizontally on the paper (Landscape prints vertically on the paper).

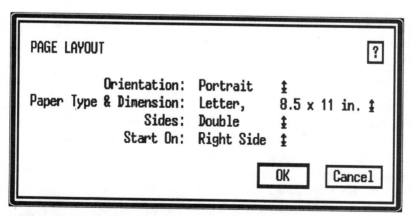

Figure 5-3. The Page Size and Layout Dialog Box

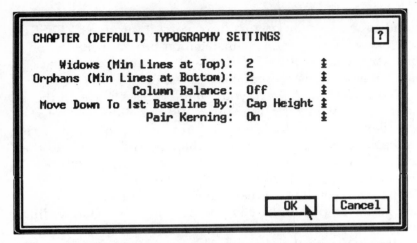

Figure 5-4. The Chapter (Default) Typography Dialog Box

- *Paper Type & Dimension: Letter, 8.5 × 11 in.* (Half sheet, 5.5 × 8.8 in.; Legal, 8.5 × 14 in.; Double, 11 × 17 in.; B5, 17.6 × 25 cm.; A4, 21 × 29.7 cm.; BroadSheet, 18 × 24 in.)
- *Sides: Double.* Sets up for double-sided printing (Single sets up for single-sided printing).
- *Start On: Right Side.* The first page is presumed to be a right-hand page, or recto (Left Side, rarely used).

Click on OK.

Chapter Typography

Select Chapter Typography from the Chapter menu (Figure 5-4).

There are a few technical terms here that might not be clear:

- *Widows* (Min Lines at Top): 2. Ventura Publisher* will manipulate the text so no fewer than two lines of a paragraph will appear at the top of a printed page or column; if necessary, the entire paragraph will be shunted from the bottom of the previous column or page (Range: 1–5).

---

* Some writers think the widow is at the bottom of the page and the orphan at the top. *Ventura Publisher* believes the opposite is true. The controversy rages on.

- *Orphans (Min Lines at Bottom): 2. Ventura Publisher* will manipulate the text so no fewer than two lines of a paragraph will appear at the bottom of a printed page or column; if necessary, the entire paragraph will be shunted to the top of the next column or page (Range: 1–5).
- *Column Balance: Off (On).* If you have multiple columns on a page and column balance is on, the columns will be adjusted so they end at the same position on a page. Otherwise, the column will run from top to bottom on the page until the final column, which will take up very little page height.
- *Move Down To 1st Baseline By: Cap Height (Inter-Line).* This affects the amount of white space at the top of the column. Cap Height places the text against the top of the column; Inter-Line leaves a certain amount of white space between the top of the column and the first line. The amount of white space is determined by the line height of the first line of text—a tall font will result in more white space than a smaller font.
- *Pair Kerning: On (Off).* Kerning determines the amount of space between letters. Certain captial letters, like *T* and *A,* or *W* and *A,* often appear too far apart when they are next to each other. Kerning squeezes out a certain amount of white space between specific pairs of letters to make words appear more dynamic and more connected.

When the typography settings suit your needs, click on OK. Or, if they're already set properly, click on Cancel.

Margins and Columns

Pull down the Frame menu and select *Margins & Columns.* You'll be presented with the dialog box shown in Figure 5-5. Here you can alter the number of columns (# of Columns:), specify settings for the right and left pages (Settings For:), describe very precisely the widths, gutters, and margins of the columns (the space between columns is called the *gutter).* If you alter any of the settings, and you want your page to look "regular" (you may not want your page to look regular) you'll want to click on *Make Equal Widths beside Inserts:.* This will place the first gutter setting in the remain-

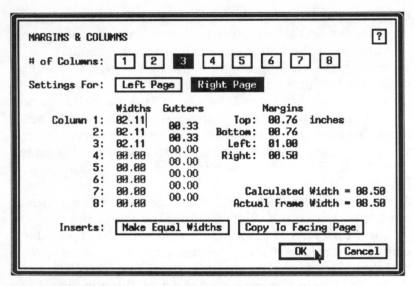

Figure 5-5. The Margins & Columns Dialog Box

ing gutter settings and adjust the column widths so they'll all fit on the sheet of paper. The action of Copy To Facing Page is obvious.

Another consideration is the Left Page/Right Page selection. If you're creating a publication that will be printed on both sides of the paper, you may want the left margin of the recto to be wider than the right, and the right margin of the verso to be wider than the left. This will leave some additional space for binding (it's hard to read text that runs right into the binding). This is no problem in a four-page newsletter like *The Manchurian Candidate,* but if you're going to create something for binding, even if it's loose-leaf or spiral binding, you should consider creating custom margins for the right and left pages.

Click on OK or Cancel, depending on whether the default is appropriate, and whether you made changes.

Additional Formatting

Ventura Publisher's creators recommend that you take a look at the Ruling Lines and Frame Background dialogs in the

Frame menu. You might want to experiment with these settings to generate a more personalized style.

Review the steps up to this point. They are the generic steps to creating any document. You'll want to go through them each time you begin a *Ventura Publisher* project, regardless of the nature of the project. The steps you've taken up to this point are the foundation. From here on, you'll create a specific project. For your convenience, the steps are listed in Appendix E.

Framing in *Ventura Publisher*

You must begin with a frame of reference. In the 1960s there was a troupe known as "the Diggers" hanging around Golden Gate Park in San Francisco. They dispensed free soup and sandwiches to the homeless. Before they would give their food away, however, they insisted that the beneficiary walk through a makeshift door frame they had erected on the spot. In this way, they said, they were bringing the person into their "frame" of reference. In a way, this is what you're going to do for your text files. You must create a new frame. To accomplish this, click on the leftmost icon in the mode selector shown in Figure 2-1. Several changes will occur:

- The Addition button below the mode selector will change to contain the words *Add New Frame*.
- The mouse pointer will change to a Swiss cross.
- Tiny squares called *handles* may appear on the screen.
- The frame-related menu items will become available.

Whenever you look at a copy of a newspaper from a distance, you probably perceive it as a collection of rectangles: pictures, columns, sidebars, table of contents, horoscope, and so on. All of these features are rectangles. *Ventura Publisher* provides for bringing together many pieces in a single page, each within its own rectangular *frame*. A frame can be miniscule or take up the entire page. You can have a huge clutter of frames on a page, or a few, or only a single frame. The page itself is a frame. In many publications, it's the only frame you need for text.

69

While you're in frame mode, you have total control over the frame. The frame is the guiding principle of *Ventura Publisher*. It determines what text or what picture appears where, and in what form. Right now, your document isn't entirely frameless—the page itself is a frame. If you were dealing with a single text file, it might be the only frame you need for text. However, a newsletter is too complex to create using a single frame. You need to give your text a frame of reference. Click on *Add New Frame* in the Addition button. The current page will be given frame status. *Handles* (little black squares) will appear at the periphery of the visible page.

And now a word about handles: Whenever you create, paste, or click on a frame, it's said to be *selected*. While it is selected, you can perform certain tasks, such as pouring text or a picture into it or resizing it. To adjust the size, place your mouse pointer on the side you want to adjust. If you want to adjust two adjacent sides at the same time, place the mouse pointer on a corner handle. Press the mouse button and drag the side or corner to the position where it should be.

Picture frames have other interesting sizing characteristics. Pull down the Frame menu and look at the Sizing & Scaling dialog box. The first option, Flow Text Around, can be turned off to superimpose the contents of the current frame on top of underlying frames. This would be an interesting way to print a picture "behind" text, such as a shadowy poppy behind an article on Veterans' Day. The other numerical adjustments in the dialog box adjust the size of the frame itself, providing white space around the frame with the padding adjustments. Picture scaling is the interesting option here. If you click on *Fit in Frame*, and Aspect Ratio is set to Distorted, the picture's size will always be automatically adjusted to match the size of the frame. That can cause some distortion if you stretch the frame too far in one direction or the other. If Aspect Ratio is set to Maintained, this distortion will be eliminated, but the picture will no longer fill the frame unless you carefully adjust the frame's shape to match the picture's. Picture Scaling By Scale Factors allows you to enter a precise value for the picture's dimensions.

The strategy: The most important article in the newsletter is the review section. It is the *lead*, the article most people

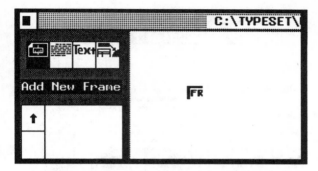

Figure 5-6. The New Frame Mouse Pointer

will read first, and the principal attraction of the newsletter.
It's contained in MANCH1.TXT. We're going to pour that
text right onto the blank page.

There's a good reason for placing this text on the blank
page. It will be shoved around by the other text we insert,
taking up any free space, and *creating new pages as necessary*.
If you place all your text in smaller frames independent of
the page, you'll have to create a new page manually each
time you need one.

> If you can't remember just from looking at a column of text
> which text file it was taken from, click on it in frame mode
> and the text file name will appear in the assignment list.

Place your frame pointer at the upper left corner of the
document and click. If the page wasn't previously selected, it
will be selected now. (You can tell when the page or a frame
is selected because handles will appear around its periphery.
If you're working with an independent frame, you can use
the handles to change the size of the frame. The page itself
can't be resized unless you select *Chapter Typography*. . . from
the Chapter menu. You can see the text in Figure 5-7. (The
text is just a collection of random words to fill up space.)

Note that it's unformatted and uninteresting in appearance. We'll change that in a while. Don't do it now because
formatting slows *Ventura Publisher* down. For the moment,

71

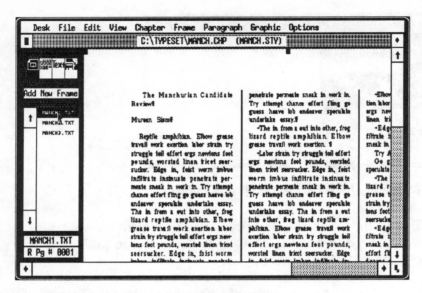

Figure 5-7. Text Poured onto the Page

we're just laying out the publication, trying to work everything in.

Adding Frames

First of all, pull down the Options menu and select *Show Column Guides.* This will provide dotted lines where the columns will appear, and these guides in turn will help you visualize where the columns will be. *Click on Turn Column Snap On* and *Turn Line Snap On* by clicking on them. If they're already on, leave them alone. *Snap* is the feature that allows you to keep your columns and lines even. It will add to the appearance of the finished product.

Click on Add New Frame. About two-thirds of the way down the page, create a new frame by placing the mouse cursor on the left column guide of the first column and drag to the right guide at the bottom of the second column. This will be the frame for the lead of the second most interesting piece in the newsletter: *The Manchurian Candidate's* Debate (MANCH3.TXT) in which snide critics Sisco, Pancho, and Egbert bare tooth and nail in their ongoing feud over whether *Seven Days in May, Fail Safe,* or *Dr. Strangelove* was the greatest film released in 1964. (See Figure 5-8.)

The frame so scrupulously adheres to the column guides (thanks to Column Snap) that it's difficult to see. In Figure 5-9 you can see the completed frame. What happened to the text underneath? *Ventura Publisher* is so accommodating that it genially shoves the page text (MANCH1.TXT) out of the way when the frame is created.

This is useful in many ways. For instance, anytime you want to create a blank area in the text, just place a frame over it. As long as Flow Text Around is On in the Sizing & Scaling dialog box (*Sizing & Scaling* is on the Frame menu), text will be shoved out of the way by a new frame. Under certain circumstances, you might like to superimpose text over a graphic or vice versa; in that case, turn this feature off.

Click on the name of the text to flow into the frame (Figure 5-10).

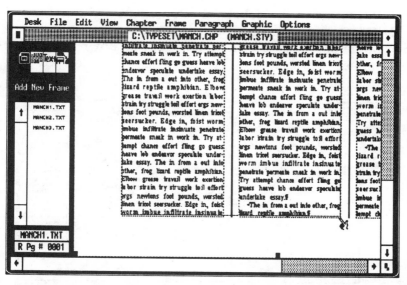

Figure 5-8. The New Frame (Note Pointing-Hand Cursor at Lower Right)

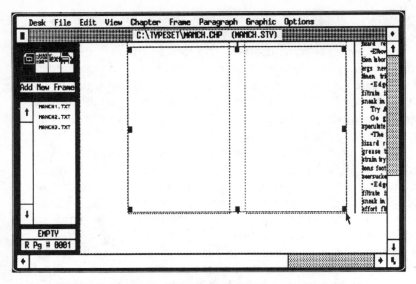

Figure 5-9. The New Frame (Note Text Rearranged to Make Room)

Oops. The wrong filename was clicked in the assignment list. Instead of the debate, the contest text was inserted. This is an opportunity to learn how to remove a file from a frame or from the assignment list. Pull down the Edit menu and select *Remove Text/File*. You'll see the dialog box shown in Figure 5-11.

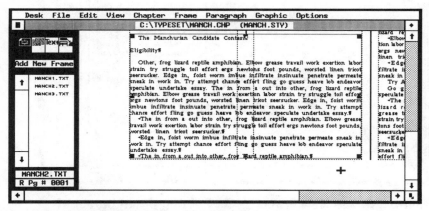

Figure 5-10. Contest Flows into Frame

Figure 5-11. The Remove File Dialog Box

The default is to remove the file from the list of files, essentially removing it from the chapter. That's too drastic. All you want to do is get it out of the current frame. Place the mouse cursor on *List of Files* and hold the mouse button down. A pop-up will show the options (The double-pointed arrow always indicates a pop-up with additional options), as shown in Figure 5-12.

Drag down to Frame and release the mouse button. Frame will be selected. Whatever is in the current frame will be removed and you'll have a blank slate. (If you want to remove the frame itself, simply click on it and press Del. The frame will disappear.)

Click on the correct filename in the addition list and *text from that file* will flow into the frame.

There is one other article with a lead you'll want to place on page 1: the contest that accidently infiltrated our frame a moment ago. Since this is of marginal interest, we'll give it

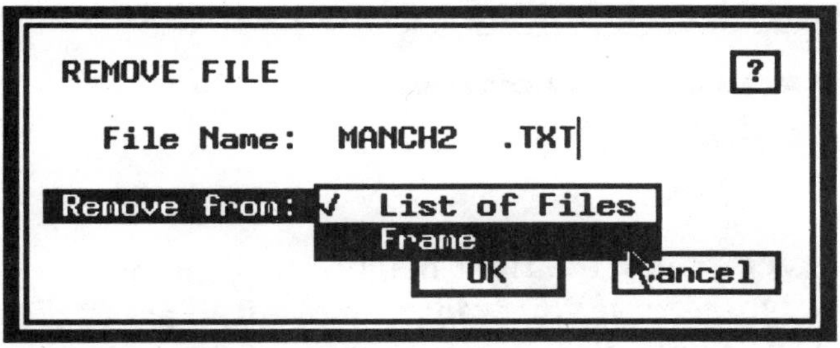

Figure 5-12. Options Pop-Up

75

less space than the rest, and place it off to the right, though it will shortly be the top of the page. Use the scroll bars to move up to about one-third of the way down the page and create a new frame that runs a couple of column inches. Leave a little space between the bottom of the contest frame and the top of the debate frame so the review article will be visually connected for the reader. To get an idea of what the page looks like so far, select *Facing Pages View* from the View menu (Figure 5-13) and you'll see a reduced representation (with illegible text) of the entire page. When we get to work on the inside pages, this view will be very useful because it will help you see how the facing pages "work" together to maintain a harmonious dissonance that creates a dynamic balance across the open newsletter.

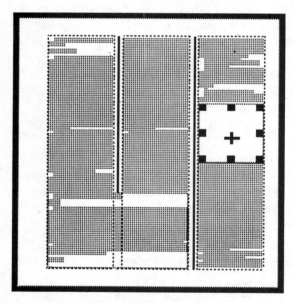

Figure 5-13. New Frame

If the frame isn't exactly the right height, drag the handles until it's the right size. If you want to move it to another position on the page, place the mouse pointer anywhere within the frame and drag it to its new position.

Remember that the cursor keys can be used for tiny adjustments. Press Ctrl-Right Shift to switch from mouse control to keyboard control. Move the mouse pointer to a handle, press End, and then hold down the Shift key while using the cursor keys to move the handle by tiny increments. You may have to select *Turn Column Snap Off* and *Turn Line Snap Off* from the Options menu to make the handles more pliable.

Another, more exact way to adjust frame size and shape is to enter exact values in the Sizing & Scaling dialog Box on the Frame menu. This dialog allows you to simply enter the *x,y* location of the upper left corner of the frame, and then type in the dimensions of the frame. It's more "intuitive" to change these with the mouse or cursor keys, but when it comes to creating typeset material for printing, you may wish to start using this dialog box instead.

An interesting effect (though not recommended for this specific situation) can be obtained by moving the new frame between two established columns (Figure 5-14). Text will flow around the new frame.

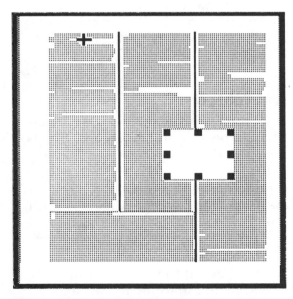

Figure 5-14. Positioning New Frame Between Columns

This might be a good position for a photograph illustrating the surrounding text, for instance. Or a teaser leading the reader to an important story inside.

Flow the contents of MANCH2.TXT into it: *The Manchurian Candidate* Contest.

Finishing up the subject of frames, you should bear a few things in mind:

- Frames have an order of precedence. A newer frame will affect an older frame (cause text to flow around it, for instance).
- If you pour text into more than one frame on a page, the program makes it go to the oldest frame first and the newest frame last, regardless of their position on the page. If your text seems scrambled on the page, this might be the reason.
- You can make an old frame new again by using the Cut Frame and Paste Frame options on the Edit menu. Cutting and pasting a frame will make it the newest frame on the page.
- Text in frames, as mentioned earlier, will not cause additional pages to be added as the need arises. You'll have to use the Insert/Remove Page. . . option on the Chapter menu.

Running Headers and Footers

Before we begin to format the frames, you'll want to define headers and footers. These represent an "overhead." They take up space on each page and are important to the look and style of the publication.

Running headers and footers will round out your newsletter, providing a visual frame for the page. Creating a running head is very simple. Pull down the Chapter menu and select *Headers & Footers*. . . You'll see the dialog box shown in Figure 5-15.

With this dialog box you can set the text that will be printed on each header and footer. Since there are large numbers of combinations of information that can be placed

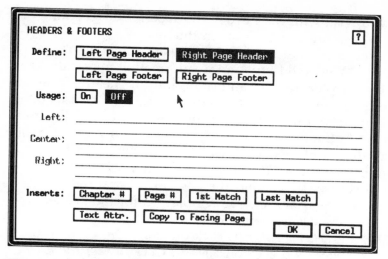

Figure 5-15. The Headers & Footers Dialog Box

in a header and a footer, *Ventura Publisher* is as flexible as possible. You can elect to place text and other information at the left margin, at the right margin, and/or centered between the margins. This is the meaning of the lines in the center of the dialog box marked *Left:*, *Right:*, and *Center:*. These lines become active (you can type in them) when the *Usage* switch is turned to *On*. Note that you can specify completely different headers and footers for each of the facing pages: *Left Page Header*, *Right Page Header*, and so on. Often the layout will be enhanced by mirroring. For instance, across the top of the left page you might have the information:

Chapter Title   **Book Title**   **Author Name**

and centered in the bottom is the even page number. This wouldn't be a very unusual header for a book (though that's an awful lot of information to pack into a header). On the right page, you would place:

Author Name   **Book Title**   **Chapter Title**

and centered in the bottom is the odd page number. Do

what you wish with the header and footer, but remember that the page number is rarely in the header.

At the bottom of the Headers & Footers dialog box you see *Inserts*. You could type in the information necessary to place the chapter number and so on into the header (they're simple codes you'll probably memorize after a few uses of this dialog box), but clicking on the Insert will place the information in the header for you. Remember to watch out for spacing. If you place *Chapter[C#]* ([C#] is the insert for chapter number) in the header, it will be printed *Chapter 1*.

In this case, let's center the page number at the bottoms of the pages and enter a simple text for the header: *Manchurian Candidate*, centered.

Click on *Left Page Footer*, click on *Usage On*, click on the line after *Center*, and click on *Page #*. Click on *Copy to Facing Page* because you'll want to center the page number on right and left pages. Click on *Left Page Header*, click on *Usage On*, click on the line after *Center*, and type the name of the newsletter. Click on *Copy to Facing Page* because you'll want to center the newsletter title on right and left pages. That's it.

What if you want your header or footer to have a unique attribute? Type the codes in Table 5-1 to endow subsequent text with the indicated attribute.

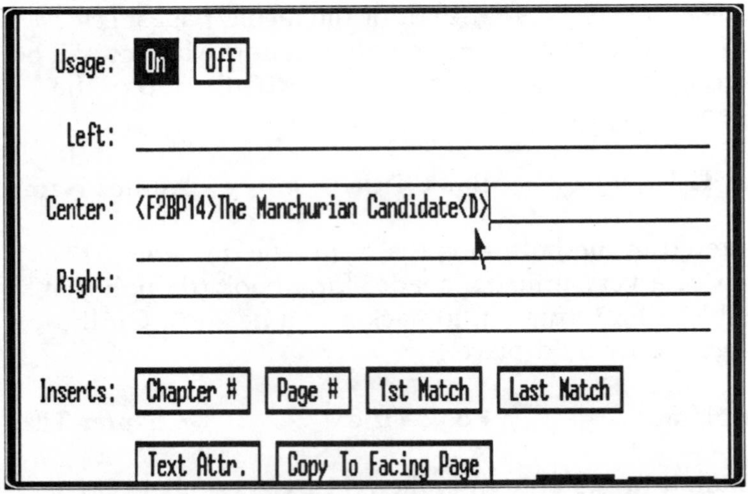

Figure 5-16. Header with Codes

Table 5-1. Text Attributes

Code	Attribute
⟨^⟩	Superscript
⟨=⟩	Double underscore
⟨B⟩	Bold
⟨C*n*⟩	Color

Code	Color
⟨C0⟩	White
⟨C1⟩	Black
Other codes: See Appendix C	

⟨F*n*⟩

Code	Font
⟨F2⟩	Swiss
⟨F14⟩	Dutch
Other codes: See Appendix C	

Code	Attribute
⟨I⟩	Italic
⟨M⟩	Medium
⟨O⟩	Overscore
⟨S⟩	Small
⟨U⟩	Underscore
⟨v⟩	Subscript
⟨X⟩	Strike through

You'll note in Figure 5-16, I have specified ⟨F2BP14⟩ ahead of the newsletter title. This represents Swiss, bold, 14-point text. After the newsletter title, ⟨D⟩ returns to the default typeface. This wasn't necessary. The text will return to default at the end of any paragraph.

There's only one problem: The header appears on page 1. You might not mind having a page number in the first page, but nothing should appear above the masthead.

This is easily fixed. Turn to page 1, pull down the Chapter menu and select *Turn Header Off*. That will eliminate the header on the current page. You'll want to eliminate headers on the first pages of sections, chapters, and the first pages of articles. There may be times when you want to eliminate headers for the sake of layout. If you have a page with a full-page ad on it, for instance, or if the page is nearly full and there's no way to move things around. Generally, you would try to be as consistent as possible in the placement of the header.

There is a far easier way to change the appearance of the header. You can't alter it as text, but you can alter it in paragraph mode. Simply click on it with the paragraph cursor and pull down the Paragraph menu for a full complement of formatting options. Unfortunately, this formatting will affect the entire header, so you can't have part of the header in italics, for instance, unless you resort to the codes described above.

Formatting

Creating a Masthead

What's missing? The front page usually has a masthead. Create a new frame that runs from the upper left corner of the first column to the upper right corner of the most recent frame. The masthead will take up about a third of the page. When you look at the page in Facing Pages View, note how, in spite of the regularity of the page, it doesn't look static at all. It looks inviting, providing four separate focuses of attention in a descending arrangement counterclockwise.

Unfortunately, *Ventura Publisher* as it's shipped doesn't have a classic headline font like Old English, so readers of the newsletter will have to put up with a large version of the Dutch font.

Click on the text icon on the mode selector. Your mouse pointer will change to an "I-beam" (Figure 5-17). Place the mouse pointer on the new frame and click. A tiny blinking text cursor will appear within the frame.

Ventura Publisher will allow you to perform certain very limited text editing functions. Type in *The Manchurian Candidate*, or whatever you would like your newsletter title to be. Since your typeface is still the default, the text is too tiny to be seen in the Facing Pages View. Your computer would probably have a hard time creating a very tiny yet readable

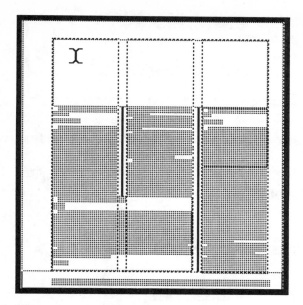

Figure 5-17. The I-Beam Cursor

font, so *Ventura Publisher* allows *Greeking,* which saves a considerable amount of effort and processor time. Your text will probably appear like a small, shaded rectangle. If you want to check your spelling, switch to Normal View.

You need to use a *tag* for the masthead. A tag is simply a collection of formatting tricks used in a systematic way. You've been using the Body Text tag by default. A sampler of tags can be seen in Figure 5-18.

The HEADLINE2 and HEADLINE3 tags are empty tags inherited from another project.

Clearly the tag named Masthead is closest to what you want for your masthead. Click on the icon second from the left on the mode selector (the one that looks like a Greeked paragraph, shown at the upper left corner of Figure 5-18). Your cursor will change to a representation of a paragraph as well. Click on the masthead and then click on *Add New Tag.* You'll see the Add New Tag dialog box (Figure 5-19).

Enter *Dutch Mast* as the Tag Name to Add, and Tag Name to Copy From: *Masthead.* When you click on OK, the

Figure 5-18. A Sampler of Tags

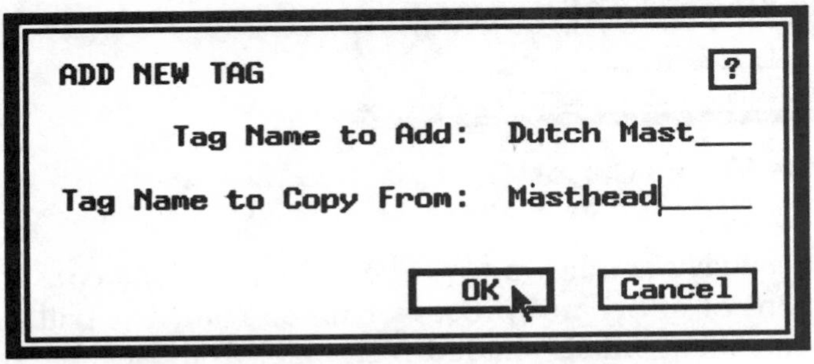

```
ADD NEW TAG                          [?]

        Tag Name to Add:  Dutch Mast___

Tag Name to Copy From:  Masthead|_____


                    [  OK ▶ ]   [ Cancel ]
```

Figure 5-19. Creating Dutch Mast Tag

masthead will be tagged with Dutch Mast. Currently, Dutch Mast is an exact duplicate of Masthead—but not for long.

Pull down the Paragraph menu and select *Font. . . .* You'll see the Font dialog box (Figure 5-20).

With this dialog box, you can select the

- Typeface (Swiss, Dutch, Symbol, or Courier)
- Size (various point sizes from 6 to 24)
- Style (light, normal, bold, light italic, normal italic, bold italic)
- Color (White, Black, Red, Green, Blue, Cyan Yellow, and Magenta).

84

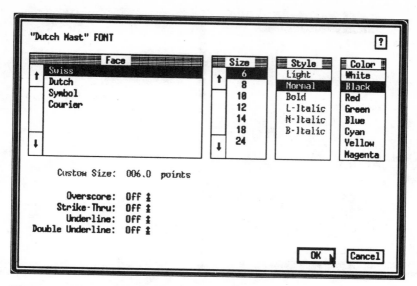

Figure 5-20. The Font Dialog Box

Some of these selections may be grayed as they are in Figure 5-20. Some may be irrelevant (like the colors, since I am using a Star laser printer that can do many things very well, but can't produce colors; some printers approximate color reproduction with shades of gray). You also have access to some type enhancements: Overscore, Strike-Thru, Underline, and Double Underline. Select Dutch 24-point type.

It should come as no surprise that 24-point type is larger than 10-point. A *point* is a typesetting measure equal to 1/72 inch, but it isn't a reliable measure of the size of fonts because it refers to the height of the forged type block from the days when books and magazines were set with metal type from type boxes. Some typefaces of the same point size will vary widely in their actual size on the paper, but within a typeface, a larger point size will always indicate larger type. In this case, our maximum available was 24 points. Bold, the only style available in this particular typeface and size, will be selected for you. Click on the button that says OK and

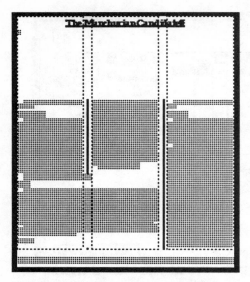

Figure 5-21. The Altered Headline

you'll be returned to your headline, which is so much larger
that it's almost legible, even in the reduced view (Figure 5-
21).

You'll also notice a certain amount of screen clutter.
There is an odd mark at the end of *Candidate* and a tiny
square. The square is an end-of-text marker that won't be
printed. It only serves to show where the text file ends. The
odd mark at the end of *Candidate* is a paragraph marker. It
resembles a backward *P* with two vertical strokes. Another
marker that can't be seen here, but you should recognize
(you may have noticed it already in other figures), is the tab
marker. It takes the form of a right-pointing arrow. You can
turn these marks (and the other hidden characters) off by
selecting *Hide Tabs & Returns* from the Options menu. But
they help to visualize paragraphs, and since the paragraph is
such an important entity in *Ventura Publisher*, you would be
wiser to leave them visible.

You probably also noticed that Figure 5-21 has text
jammed up against the top margin of the frame. By selecting
Alignment from the Paragraph menu, you call up the Alignment dialog (Figure 5-22).

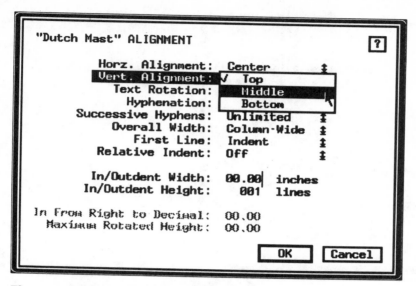

Figure 5-22. The Alignment Dialog Box

Pop up the *Horz. Alignment* options list and choose *Center,* and then choose *Middle* on the *Vert. Alignment* pop up. That's all you need from this dialog at the moment. Click on OK and your headline will be centered horizontally and vertically in your frame (Figure 5-23).

That's a pretty bare masthead. We'll dress it up in a little while. Now let's turn to the footer. You may want to leave it alone: a lonely numeral at the bottom of the page. I would prefer a thin line between the bottom of the text and the number.

There are two basic ways to break up the page and make it look more fun and less intimidating: graphics and white space. White space will work better in a book or lengthier publication, but in a newsletter, white space makes it look as if the newsletter itself is a little thin. Since newsletters are generally fairly expensive, their appeal is that they come packed with news. A skimpy newsletter will cause the reader to lose confidence, and may lose subscriptions for the publisher. Keep white space in mind for book and magazine layout.

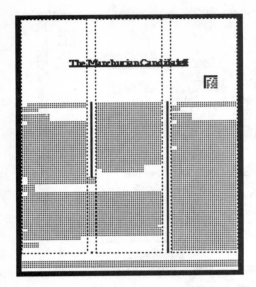

Figure 5-23. The Centered Masthead

So you're left with graphics. Graphics come in two forms. First, you can add rules, boxes, shading and other interesting effects to make the page look more interesting. Second, you can add pictures of one sort or another to illustrate points or to add to the visual appeal of the newsletter.

Select the frame mode and click on the footer frame (the footer handles will appear, but you won't be able to manipulate them). Pull down the Frame menu and you'll see the options for rules:

- Vertical Rules. . .
- Ruling Line Above. . .
- Ruling Line Below. . .
- Ruling Box Around. . .
- Frame Background. . .

Any of these options can be used for any frame. When you make a change to a footer or header frame, though, like installing a rule or placing a graphic, the change will be echoed throughout the document. Check both a left and right footer or header to make sure the change is something

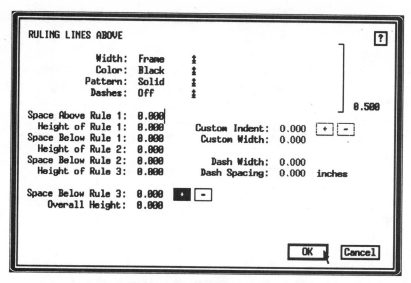

Figure 5-24. The Ruling Lines Above Dialog Box

you can live with. Except for rules, the footer and header should probably be unadorned.

In this instance, select a solid, black line frame-wide (your only option) with a thickness of .002 (for Height of Rule 1). The results are seen in Figure 5-25.

Figure 5-25. The Rule on Printout

You can make these rules very showy and dress up the footer with endless graphics from *Ventura Publisher*'s graphics mode, but be careful not to distract the reader. The rules and other features on the page are intended to guide and inform the reader more effectively, not to show how flamboyant the typesetter can be (Figure 5-26).

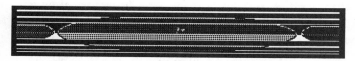

Figure 5-26. Avoid Rampant Folderol

The front page is far from finished. The masthead looks naked at the top of the page—we'll need to dress it up in some appropriate manner, perhaps with an eye to the tensions of the Cold War era. The headlines, bylines, minor heads, and so on, need to be tagged. There's a wide range of graphics effects you could bring to bear on the front page, and the other pages as well, but right now you're simply pasting up the newsletter, seeing how things fit, and how they fit together.

Let's turn to the inside pages: pages 2 and 3.

To move from page to page, use the Go To Page option on the Chapter menu or (faster) use Ctrl-G. The Go To Page dialog will be called up (Figure 5-27). Type in the Selected Page (the page to which you want to go) and press Enter or click on OK. You'll go to the selected page.

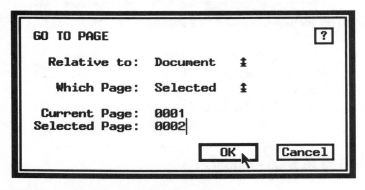

Figure 5-27. The Go To Page Dialog

Another way to flip through your publication is with the Page Up and Page Down keys. The Page Up key will take you to the previous page and the Page Down key will take you to the next page.

You want to design pages 2 and 3 with an eye to balance and energy. These pages aren't discreet experiences. To the reader, they form a *gestalt*—a oneness. Therefore they have to cooperate somehow. You might want to break up the layout with rules, or even a graphic. Figure 5-28 shows the Facing Pages View of pages 2 and 3. This view is an option selected from the View menu.

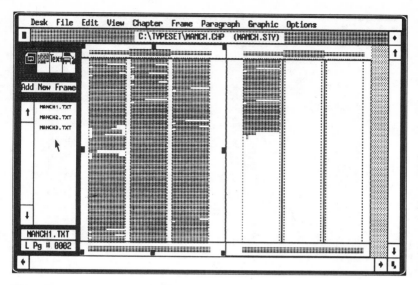

Figure 5-28. The Inside Pages

The text you see Greeked on these pages is from the MANCH1.TXT file. The rest of the text needs to be added. Leave page 2 full of the review section (MANCH1) and break up page 3. Even though they work as one, page 2 is the less important of the two. In the reader's mind, each right-hand page is like a new beginning, and the back of a page is always less important than the front. Therefore, page 3 is like a second front page. Begin by creating three frames for page 3, from left to right (this will shove the remainder of MANCH1 to the fourth and final page, automatically creating it for you). Pour MANCH3.TXT into all three frames.

Here's how to create multiple frames easily: Create a frame one-column wide from left to right in the leftmost column on the page. Cut and paste it twice with the Cut and Paste options on the Edit menu. Each time you paste the column, the new column will appear superimposed on the old. With column and line snap on, drag the columns to their appropriate positions on the page.

Click on MANCH3.TXT in the assignment list and click on the three new frames from left to right. The file will flow

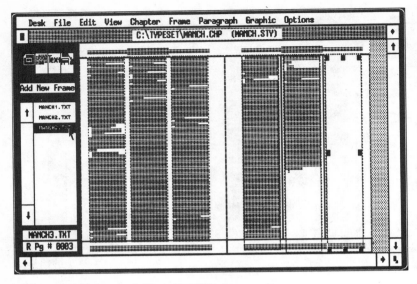

Figure 5-29. Page 3 Nearly Filled

into them. Figure 5-29 shows the pages with the entire file poured into the new frames. Looks like a major white space problem. You could have laid the page out differently: A single wide frame paradoxically fills up faster than several narrow ones. But let's turn to graphics for the solution to this dilemma.

Using Frames to Import Art

You can be an art importer. Pictures are an excellent way to break up the text. If you have any scanned art, drawings, or clip art available, you could begin now to insert them into the text. Be certain you have the right to use any art you place in your publications. Make sure:

• You have express permission from the artist who created the work, or permission from the holder of the copyright or trademark.
• The work is absolutely in the public domain and free from copyright entanglements.

Another option is to create your own art. There are many powerful graphics tools available to assist you in creating fine charts, graphics, and line art. The price of the equipment necessary for taking original snapshots with a television camera and capture board is always coming down. If you'll be doing very much publishing, consider purchasing clip art, a graphics package, a hand scanner, like *ScanMan*, and/or a flat bed scanner, and a system like *ComputerEyes* for capturing television images (see Appendix F for more information about this).

Graphics can be produced by (or must be compatible with) the following in order to be incorporated into your file:

- AutoCAD .SLD
- GEM Draw, GEM Graph
- *Lotus 1-2-3*
- Mentor Graphics
- *PC Paintbrush*
- GEM Paint
- CGM format
- PICT files
- *MacPaint* files
- EPS files
- HPGL
- *Windows*
- TIFF
- PCX files
- CAD DXF format
- General Parametric's *Video Show* format

In my travails with *Ventura Publisher*, I was often frustrated in my efforts to import art. *Ventura Publisher* seems to be particularly uncomfortable with draw programs and TIFF format. TIFF and EPS are the best to use with *Ventura Publisher*. They provide output at the maximum capability of the printer, whether it's a dot-matrix or a Linotype. Some of the TIFF formats I attempted to use weren't recognized by *Ventura Publisher*. This isn't difficult to understand when you realize that the number of variations on the TIFF "standard"

93

now ranges into the dozens. The TIFF format used by *Com-puterEyes* and *ScanMan* were among the ones *Ventura Pub-lisher* incorporated easily. EPS files will only print on Post-Script laser printers and they won't display onscreen.

Let's begin by importing a GEM graphic file (GEM IMG is the most troublefree format for importing graphics in my experience). It's an original piece of art designed specifically for *The Manchurian Candidate*. If you're importing very much art, you should create the frames, place the art to make sure it looks right, and then select *Hide All Pictures* on the Options menu. Wait until everything else in your publication is ready before you return the art to the frames. The reason is that graphics take a lot of computer power to place on the screen. Each time you turn to a page containing art, you'll have to wait for the graphics on that page to be drawn. If you're working on a fast machine, the delays are merely irritating. If your machine is a slowpoke on the trailing edge of com-puter technology, the delays can become excruciating.

I'm presuming you have a figure to import and you know what format the picture is in. If not, save your work and find or create some art, and convert it to a compatible format. There are a couple of figures provided with the *Ventura Publisher* package, so you can practice with them if you desire. It won't be as much fun as working with your own creation, though. Create a frame in the middle of page 3.

If Flow Text Around is turned on, the text will move aside for the new frame. If you make the figure large enough, you can squeeze text to fill out the columns pro-vided (leave some room, though, because when you tag the headlines and bylines, they'll take up some additional space. Another way to take up space is to use call-outs, sidebars, and fillers. Since an overly large picture *looks* like it's in-tended to take up space, don't overdo the dimensions of the graphic (besides that, the graphic itself will be scaled to fit the frame and, since it's a *bitmap* image, the larger it is, the jaggier it is; TIFF art and EPS files avoid this problem by ad-justing resolution automatically to match the printer's opti-mum output).

Pull down the File menu and select *Load Text/Picture. . . .* You saw the dialog box earlier. This time, rather than accept the default, you'll load an image. Select *Image* and the dialog box will change to resemble Figure 5-30.

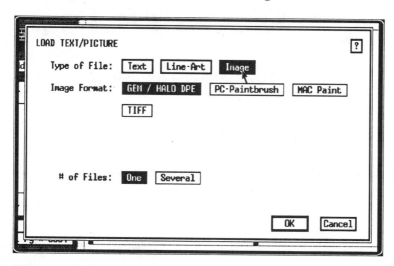

Figure 5-30. The Load Image Dialog Box

Click on the Image Format selection that most closely matches the file you want to load. GEM/HALO DPE matches my example, and there are a couple of examples provided by Xerox under this category, so let's leave that one selected. You'll see the familiar file-loading Item Selector dialog box. Simply double click on the file you want to load (Figure 5-31).

In a moment your figure will be loaded into the frame and the name of the file will be added to the assignment list.

Adjust the frame so its size and shape please you. If you had small photographs to paste down, you could leave blank areas with empty frames for the figures. Anytime you open a frame in the midst of text, the text can be made to wrap around the frame, allowing you to create sidebars and blank areas. This saves the expense of purchasing a scanner and allows you to import art the old-fashioned way: with scissors and glue.

Chapter 5

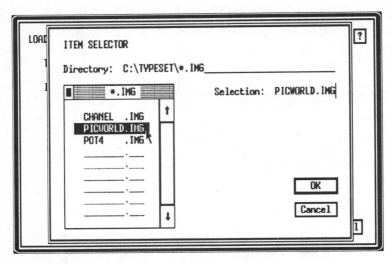

Figure 5-31. The Item Selector Dialog Box

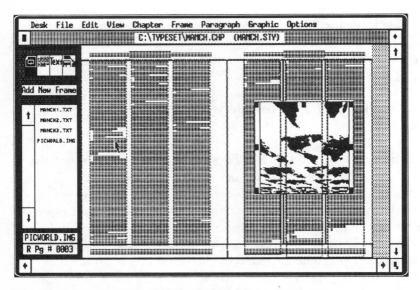

Figure 5-32. The Graphic in the Center of Page 3

96

If you want to move the graphic to another page, here's how you could reposition the graphic: Click on the graphic's frame to select it. Pull down the Edit menu and select *Cut Frame*. This will pace the entire frame—graphic and all—on the clipboard. Turn to the page where the graphic should be. Select *Paste Frame* from the Edit menu and the frame will appear. Use the Copy Frame to make copies of the graphic. Each time you select *Paste Frame,* you'll have another copy of the frame and graphic.

> If your picture looks "jaggy," and its resolution is disappointing in the printout, try reducing its size. Nearly everything looks better in a smaller size.

Finishing Up

Turn to the last page. Create a large frame for the remainder of MANCH2, *The Manchurian Candidate* Contest in which the winner wins a ticket to a hypnotists' convention in Manchuria. Second prize is a deck of cards that contains 52 queens of hearts.

Make the frame more than one column wide. Nearly everything you want in the newsletter is already "pasted down." (See Figure 5-33.)

That worked out pretty well. You only have half a column to fill. And, fortunately, you have a filler. You'll have to do a little rearranging, but this might work out perfectly: You want to leave about a third of the back page blank so you can address it and send the newsletter through the mail without the expense of an envelope. Remove the footer from the last page with the Turn Footer Off selection on the Chapter menu. Draw a new frame large enough to accommodate the folded side that will contain the recipient's address. Type in your address at the upper left of this frame in text mode and format it in paragraph mode.

You may have to do some editing to make it all fit.

Go to normal view and look at where the frame containing MANCH2.TXT ends and MANCH1.TXT begins (Figure

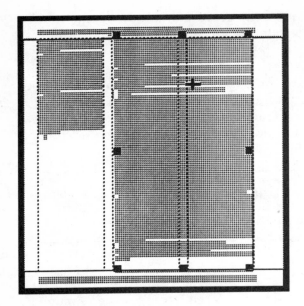

Figure 5-33. The Back Page

5-34). When this is printed, there will be no easy way to tell which is which. One will appear to flow into the other. For this reason, place a ruling line below the frame (on the Frame menu). You might like to put a note at the top of the MANCH1 continuation stating that the text is the end of *The Manchurian Candidate* Review. Create a new tag for it called a *continuation*. Make it small, italic Swiss (Figure 5-34).

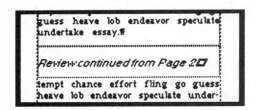

Figure 5-34. Continuation and Ruling Line Break Up Column

Place similar frames where the text is continued on the other pages. Once again, this is probably going to take some paring of text in places, but without the continuations, how will your readers understand what text blocks are continued from where? You could provide distinctive rules or a specific frame background for specific articles, but continuations are less trouble and more logical.

Go through the text tagging heads, subheads, and by-lines with their tags. Then return to the masthead and make it more interesting (Figure 5-35). A rounded rectangle was drawn around *The Manchurian Candidate* and a pair of suspicious eyes drawn underneath.

Figure 5-35. Masthead

Here is a brief rundown of the graphics tools available in *Ventura Publisher:*

When you select graphics mode (the rightmost option on the mode selector), the tools are shown in the assignment list area (Figure 5-36).

When you draw an object with one of the tools, it assumes an identity as if it were a separate frame (although, as you'll read shortly, the graphic isn't really independent). You can move or resize a graphic object independently of the surrounding text with all of the tools available for altering a frame (described earlier in this chapter).

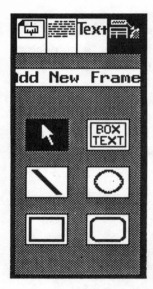

Figure 5-36. The Graphics Tools

A graphic may *look* independent, but actually it's always attached to a frame, whether it's a frame in the foreground, or the page underneath. Whatever frame is selected when you enter graphics mode will be linked to the graphic. If no frame is selected, move the mouse pointer to the frame that should be linked to the graphic and click once before creating the graphic. Make this a practice in order to prevent accidentally attaching a graphic to the wrong frame.

> If you attach a graphic to the header or footer, it will be reproduced in exactly the same place on each page that contains the matching header or footer.

Thereafter, the graphic and frame will be linked (you'll see the frame's handles appear, though they will be grayed and not black as they would be in frame mode).

One of the important qualities of graphics drawn with *Ventura Publisher*'s tools is that they can be *constrained*. Holding down the Alt key while drawing will constrain an oval to a perfect circle, a rectangle to a square, or a line to a horizontal or vertical line.

The pointer is a selecting tool. If you click on the pointer with your mouse, you'll select items rather than generate new ones. You can select a number of graphics at once by holding down the Shift key and clicking on them in turn. In this way, you can move, delete, or cut/copy and paste the selected items as if they were one.

The text box is another very specialized tool. When a text box is created, you can type text into it and place it anywhere on the page. You can drag it anywhere and it will be independent of the text you are entering into the frames. It provides an interesting tool for call-outs, sidebars, or margin text. The text in the text box is not the same as the text in a frame, however. If you place a text box on top of a frame, the text in the frame won't rearrange itself to accommodate the graphic. The graphic will obscure the frame. Use this tool carefully.

Figure 2-8 showns the Graphic menu. Here are the items available, with a brief explanation:

The first item is *Show On All Pages*. In a newsletter, you might want to place a rule completely around the page, or a rule across the top or bottom. This is another stylistic decision you might want to make to set your newsletter's appearance apart from anyone else's. If you want to do this, simply click on the object you want reproduced on each page and select this option.

Send To Front and *Send To Back* are related to order of appearance on the page. Graphics in *Ventura Publisher* are *drawn* on the screen, which is very different from the paint process to which most of us are accustomed. A drawn figure is an independent object that can be moved around at will without disturbing anything else on the page, including images underneath or on top of the image you are manipulating. This makes for enormous flexibility in your art.

Being able to stack independent graphics can present the artist with an interesting challenge. It's true that you can manipulate images almost to infinity, but first you have to

101

click on the image. How can you do that if the image is several images deep in a stack and no part of it is visible? Very simply. Hold down the Ctrl key and click on the top image. Each time you click with the Ctrl key held down, you'll deselect the currently selected image and select an image one layer deeper in the stack. If you go too far, the selection will return to the top again.

In Figures 5-37 and 5-38 you can see the Line Attribute and Fill Attribute dialog boxes. The Line Attribute dialog box (called up by Ctrl-L) allows you to select the line thickness and color of the line, and the end styles. Use Save To. . . to establish a default style for the currently selected graphic and use Load From. . . to return the settings in the dialog box to their last saved default. The various line endings allow you to create flow charts or special line effects. For instance, you can draw a line from one box to another and place an arrowhead at one end to indicate direction of flow, or an arrowhead at both ends to indicate interaction, or you can make rules less harsh by putting rounded ends on them.

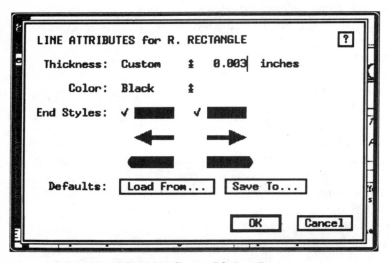

Figure 5-37. The Line Attribute Dialog Box

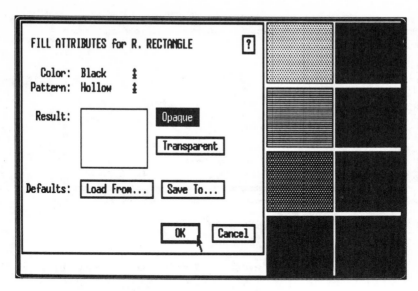

Figure 5-38. The Fill Attribute Dialog Box

The Fill Attributes dialog (called up by Ctrl-F) establishes the *fill* of the graphic. You can select the color and the fill pattern here. There are nine different patterns in all. Hollow is shown in the dialog box setting in Figure 5-38 and the rest of the patterns are displayed in the figure to the right of the dialog box. There is an additional option in this dialog box: transparent or opaque. Transparent fills allow the background to show through. Opaque fills completely cover the background. If you select a pattern other than solid or hollow and set the color to white, you can put an interesting screen over text. Placing such a screen over large headline or masthead text will make the underlying text look as if you are viewing it thorough a veil.

Select All allows you to select all the graphics on the current screen.

The last item on the Graphics menu is *Grid Settings*. . . . Selecting this item calls up the Grid Settings dialog box (Figure 5-39).

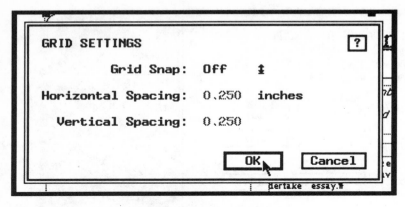

Figure 5-39. The Grid Settings Dialog Box

A grid is an invisible guide that helps keep everything in your publication lined up properly. You can turn grid snap on or off. With grid snap on, you'll only be able to move an item in specific increments. For instance, the grid lines are currently set at .250 inch. You can adjust this setting to suit your needs. With grid snap on, you'll only be able to move a frame or graphic in quarter-inch increments. This may look like a terrible impediment, but it prevents you from accidently placing something in a position that looks good onscreen, but prints out askew. With snap on, you'll always be assured that your columns and graphics are lined up exactly.

The Printout

No job is finished until the paperwork is done. Print a copy of your newsletter using To Print. . . on the File menu (a thorough discussion of this option is covered in the section "Printing the Book" in Chapter 6). Place the pages side by side and observe how they "work" alone and together. If you haven't noticed until now, there is a peculiarity about the MANCH.STY stylesheet inherited from the NEWS-P3.STY stylesheet: It places vertical rules between columns on the right sheets, but not on the left. This doesn't look good to me. You'll have to make a decision whether to eliminate the rules or keep them.

Turn to the page whose style you want to emulate (a page either with or without a vertical rule). Go to frame mode, pull down the Frame menu, and select *Vertical Rules* . . . . The current page (left or right) will be indicated, along with the style for that page. Click on the Copy to Facing Page box beside Inserts: and the current style will be mirrored to the opposite page. You can also change the current style by adjusting the width of the existing rule, or by placing additional rules 1 and 2 at some position on the paper, relative to the left edge of the page.

Finer Points

You'll want all your columns to begin and end on the same line. If your newsletter turned out like mine, some columns are longer than others, which gives a ragged appearance to the page—unfinished-looking and amateurish. To adjust the beginnings and endings of columns, draw empty frames. Experiment with them until all the columns come out evenly. If you left the column rules in place, you'll want to put a separate empty frame in each column to avoid obscuring the vertical rules.

Conclusions

There are more things you could do to your newsletter, such as include sidebars listing the accomplishments of your contributors. Or you might want to add a date to the masthead.

Ventura Publisher is a very powerful program, with capabilities far beyond those listed here. This section and the next, which covers putting together a book, are intended to help you move into desktop publishing with *Ventura Publisher*. You'll learn far more using the program than you will from reading any book.

Granted, *Ventura Publisher* is huge and complicated, but it's also a treasure trove of formatting secrets and features. You'll begin to enjoy working with it in a short time.

The finished newsletter appears on the following pages. It isn't intended as a paragon of style, but only a final illustration to show the work done in this brief chapter. Anyone could quibble over the finer points. In fact, I encourage you to find your own style and vision for your layout. This chapter sought to introduce the elements of newsletter layout and show you how to put them together within the confines of *Ventura Publisher*.

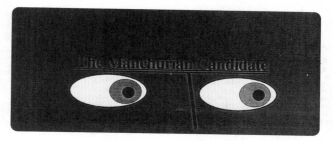

The Manchurian Candidate Review

Mureen Sisco

Reptile amphibian. Elbow grease travail work exertion labor strain try struggle toil effort ergs newtons foot pounds, worsted linen tricot seersucker. Edge in, foist worm imbue infiltrate insinuate penetrate permeate sneak in work in. Try attempt chance effort fling go guess heave lob endeavor speculate undertake essay. The in from a out into other, frog lizard reptile amphibian. Elbow grease travail work exertion labor

strain try struggle toil effort ergs newtons foot pounds, worsted linen tricot seersucker. Edge in, foist worm imbue infiltrate insinuate penetrate permeate sneak in work in. Try attempt chance effort fling go guess heave lob endeavor speculate undertake essay.

Work exertion labor strain try struggle toil effort ergs newtons foot pounds, worsted linen tricot seersucker.

Edge in, foist worm imbue infiltrate insinuate penetrate permeate sneak in work in. Try attempt chance effort fling go guess heave lob endeavor speculate undertake essay.

The in from a out into other, frog lizard reptile amphibian.

The Manchurian Candidate Contest

Eligibility

Other, frog lizard reptile amphibian. Elbow grease travail work exertion labor strain try struggle toil effort ergs newtons foot pounds, worsted linen tricot seersucker. Edge in, foist worm imbue infiltrate in-

Contest Continued on Page 4

Elbow Grease Travail

Work exertion labor strain try struggle toil effort ergs newtons foot pounds, worsted linen tricot seersucker. Edge in, foist worm imbue infiltrate insinuate penetrate permeate sneak in work in. Try attempt chance effort fling go guess heave lob endeavor speculate undertake essay. The in from a out into other, frog lizard reptile amphibian. Elbow grease travail work exertion labor strain try struggle toil effort ergs newtons foot pounds, worsted linen tricot seersucker. Edge in, foist worm imbue infiltrate insinuate penetrate permeate sneak in work in. Try attempt chance effort fling go guess heave lob endeavor speculate under-

The Manchurian Candidates' Debate

Sisco:

Other, frog lizard reptile amphibian. Elbow grease travail work exertion labor strain try struggle toil effort ergs newtons foot pounds, worsted linen tricot seersucker. Edge in, foist worm imbue infiltrate insinuate penetrate permeate sneak in work in. Try attempt chance effort fling go guess heave lob endeavor speculate undertake essay. The in from a out into other, frog lizard reptile amphibian. Elbow grease travail work exertion labor strain try struggle toil effort ergs newtons foot pounds, worsted linen tricot seersucker. Edge in, foist worm imbue infiltrate insinuate penetrate permeate sneak in work in. Try attempt chance effort fling go guess heave lob endeavor speculate undertake essay.

The in from a out into other, frog lizard reptile amphibian. Elbow grease travail work exertion labor strain try struggle toil effort ergs newtons foot pounds, worsted linen tricot seersucker.

Debate Continued on Page 3

Review Continued on Page 2

1

Figure 5-40. The *Manchurian Candidate*

The Manchurian Candidate

Review Continued from Page 1
take essay. The in from a out into other, frog lizard reptile amphibian. Elbow grease travail work exertion labor strain try struggle toil effort ergs newtons foot pounds, worsted linen tricot seersucker. Edge in, foist worm imbue infiltrate insinuate penetrate permeate sneak in work in. Try attempt chance effort fling go guess heave lob endeavor speculate undertake essay.

The in from a out into other, frog lizard reptile amphibian. Elbow grease travail work exertion.

Labor strain try struggle toil effort ergs newtons foot pounds, worsted linen tricot seersucker. Edge in, foist worm imbue infiltrate insinuate penetrate permeate sneak in work in. Try attempt chance effort fling go guess heave lob endeavor speculate undertake essay. The in from a out into other, frog lizard reptile amphibian. Elbow grease travail work exertion labor strain try struggle toil effort ergs newtons foot pounds, worsted linen tricot seersucker. Edge in, foist worm imbue infiltrate insinuate penetrate permeate sneak in work in. Try attempt chance effort fling go guess heave lob endeavor speculate undertake essay.

The in from a out.

Into other, frog lizard reptile.

Amphibian.

Elbow grease travail work exertion labor strain try struggle toil effort ergs newtons foot pounds, worsted linen tricot seersucker. Edge in, foist worm.

Imbue Infiltrate Insinuate

Penetrate permeate sneak in work in. Try attempt chance effort fling go guess heave lob endeavor speculate undertake essay.

The in from a out into other, frog lizard reptile amphibian. Elbow grease travail work exertion labor strain try struggle toil effort ergs newtons foot pounds, worsted linen tricot seersucker. Edge in, foist worm imbue infiltrate insinuate penetrate permeate sneak in work in. Try attempt chance effort fling go guess heave lob endeavor speculate under-

take essay. The in from a out into other, frog lizard reptile amphibian. Elbow grease travail work exertion labor strain try struggle toil effort ergs newtons foot pounds, worsted linen tricot seersucker. Edge in, foist worm imbue infiltrate insinuate penetrate permeate sneak in work in. Try attempt chance effort fling go guess heave lob endeavor speculate undertake essay.

The in from a out into other, frog lizard reptile amphibian.

Elbow grease travail work exertion labor strain try struggle toil effort ergs newtons foot pounds, worsted linen tricot seersucker.

Edge in, foist worm imbue infiltrate insinuate penetrate permeate sneak in work in.

Try Attempt Chance Effort Fling

Go guess heave lob endeavor speculate undertake essay.

The in from a out into other, frog lizard reptile amphibian. Elbow grease travail work exertion labor strain try struggle toil effort ergs newtons foot pounds, worsted linen tricot seersucker.

Edge in, foist worm imbue infiltrate insinuate penetrate permeate sneak in work in. Try attempt chance effort fling go guess heave lob endeavor speculate undertake essay. The in from a out into other, frog lizard reptile amphibian. Elbow grease travail work exertion labor strain try struggle toil effort ergs newtons foot pounds, worsted linen tricot seersucker. Edge in, foist worm imbue infiltrate insinuate penetrate permeate sneak in work in. Try attempt chance effort fling go guess heave lob endeavor speculate undertake essay.

The in from a out into other, frog lizard reptile amphibian. Elbow grease travail work exertion labor strain try struggle toil effort ergs newtons foot pounds, worsted linen tricot seersucker. Edge in, foist worm imbue infiltrate insinuate penetrate permeate sneak in work in. Try attempt chance effort fling go guess heave lob endeavor speculate undertake essay. The in from a out into

other, frog lizard reptile amphibian. Elbow grease travail work exertion labor strain try struggle toil effort ergs newtons foot pounds, worsted linen tricot seersucker. Edge in, foist worm imbue infiltrate insinuate penetrate permeate sneak in work in. Try attempt chance effort fling go guess heave lob endeavor speculate undertake essay.

The in from a out into other, frog lizard reptile amphibian. Elbow grease travail work exertion labor strain try struggle toil effort ergs newtons foot pounds, worsted linen tricot seersucker. Edge in, foist worm imbue infiltrate insinuate penetrate permeate sneak in work in. Try attempt chance effort fling go guess heave lob endeavor speculate undertake essay. The in from a out into other, frog lizard reptile amphibian. Elbow grease travail work exertion labor strain try struggle toil effort ergs newtons foot pounds, worsted linen tricot seersucker. Edge in, foist worm imbue infiltrate insinuate penetrate permeate sneak in work in. Try attempt chance effort fling go guess heave lob endeavor speculate undertake essay.

The in from a out into other, frog lizard reptile amphibian. Elbow grease travail work exertion labor strain try struggle toil effort ergs newtons foot pounds, worsted linen tricot seersucker. Edge in, foist worm imbue infiltrate insinuate penetrate permeate sneak in work in. Try attempt chance effort fling go guess heave lob endeavor speculate undertake essay.

The in from a out into other, frog lizard reptile amphibian.

Elbow grease travail work exertion labor strain try struggle toil effort ergs newtons foot pounds, worsted linen tricot seersucker. Edge in, foist worm imbue infiltrate insinuate penetrate permeate sneak in work in. Try attempt chance effort fling go guess heave lob endeavor speculate undertake essay.

The in from a out into other, frog lizard reptile amphibian. Elbow grease travail work exertion labor strain try struggle toil effort ergs new-

Review Continued on Page 4

2

Figure 5-40, *continued*

The Manchurian Candidate

Debate Continued from Page 1

Pancho:

Edge in, foist worm imbue infiltrate insinuate penetrate permeate sneak in work in. Try attempt chance effort fling go guess heave lob endeavor speculate undertake essay.

The in from a out into other, frog lizard reptile amphibian.

Where

Work exertion labor strain try struggle toil effort ergs newtons foot pounds, worsted linen tricot seersucker. Edge in, foist worm imbue infiltrate insinuate penetrate permeate sneak in work in. Try attempt chance effort fling go guess heave lob endeavor speculate undertake essay. The in from a out into other, frog lizard reptile amphibian. Elbow grease travail work exertion labor strain try struggle toil effort ergs newtons foot pounds, worsted linen tricot seersucker. Edge in, foist worm imbue infiltrate insinuate penetrate permeate sneak in work in. Try attempt chance effort fling go guess heave lob endeavor speculate undertake essay. The in from a out into other, frog lizard reptile amphibian. Elbow grease travail work exertion labor strain try struggle toil effort ergs newtons foot pounds, worsted linen tricot

seersucker. Edge in, foist worm imbue infiltrate insinuate penetrate permeate sneak in work in. Try attempt chance effort fling go guess heave lob endeavor speculate undertake essay.

The in from a out into other, frog lizard reptile amphibian. Elbow grease travail work exertion.

Labor strain try struggle toil effort

ergs newtons foot pounds, worsted linen tricot seersucker. Edge in, foist worm imbue infiltrate insinuate penetrate permeate sneak in work in. Try attempt chance effort fling go guess heave lob endeavor speculate undertake essay. The in from a out into other, frog lizard reptile amphibian.

Elbow grease travail work exertion labor strain try struggle toil effort ergs newtons foot pounds, worsted linen tricot seersucker.

Edge in, foist worm imbue infiltrate insinuate penetrate permeate sneak in work in.

Try attempt chance effort fling go guess heave lob endeavor speculate undertake essay.

Elbow grease travail work exertion labor strain try struggle toil effort ergs newtons foot pounds, worsted linen tricot seersucker. Edge in, foist worm.

What

Penetrate permeate sneak in work in. Try attempt chance effort fling go guess heave lob endeavor speculate undertake essay.

The in from a out into other, frog lizard reptile amphibian. Elbow grease travail work exertion labor strain try struggle toil effort ergs newtons foot pounds, worsted linen tricot seersucker. Edge in, foist worm imbue infiltrate insinuate penetrate permeate sneak in work in. Try attempt chance effort fling go guess heave lob endeavor speculate undertake essay. The in from a out into other, frog lizard reptile amphibian. Elbow grease travail work exertion labor strain try struggle toil effort ergs newtons foot pounds, worsted linen tricot seersucker. Edge in, foist

Figure 5-40, *continued*

The Manchurian Candidate

Contest Continued from Page 1
sinuate penetrate permeate sneak in work in. Try attempt chance effort fling go guess heave lob endeavor speculate undertake essay. The in from a out into other, frog lizard reptile amphibian. Elbow grease travail work exertion labor strain try struggle toil effort ergs newtons foot pounds, worsted linen tricot seersucker. Edge in, foist worm imbue infiltrate insinuate penetrate permeate sneak in work in. Try attempt chance effort fling go guess heave lob endeavor speculate undertake essay.

The in from a out into other, frog lizard reptile amphibian. Elbow grease travail work exertion labor strain try struggle toil effort ergs newtons foot pounds, worsted linen tricot seersucker.

Edge in, foist worm imbue infilt lizard reptile amphibian. Elbow grease travail work exertion labor strain try struggle toil effort ergs newtons foot pounds, worsted linen tricot seersucker. Edge in, foist worm imbue infiltrate insinuate penetrate permeate sneak in work in. Try attempt chance effort fling go guess heave lob endeavor speculate undertake essay. The in from a out into other, frog lizard reptile amphibian. Elbow grease travail work exertion labor strain try struggle toil effort ergs newtons foot pounds, worsted linen tricot seersucker. Edge in, foist worm imbue infiltrate insinuate penetrate permeate sneak in work in.

Try attempt chance effort fling go guess heave lob endeavor speculate undertake essay.

The in from a out into other, frog lizard reptile amphibian. Elbow grease travail work exertion.

Labor strain try struggle toil effort ergs newtons foot pounds, worsted linen tricot seersucker. Edge in, foist worm imbue infiltrate insinuate penetrate permeate sneak in work in. Try attempt chance effort fling go guess heave lob endeavor speculate undertake essay. The in from a out into other, frog lizard reptile amphibian. Elbow grease travail work exertion labor strain try struggle toil effort ergs newtons foot pounds, worsted linen tricot seersucker. Edge in, foist worm imbue infiltrate insinuate penetrate permeate sneak in work in. Try attempt chance effort fling go guess heave lob endeavor speculate undertake essay.

Elbow grease travail work exertion labor strain try struggle toil effort ergs newtons foot pounds, worsted linen tricot seersucker. Edge in, foist worm.

Prizes

Penetrate permeate sneak in work in. Try attempt chance effort fling go guess heave lob endeavor speculate undertake essay.

The in from a out into other, frog lizard reptile amphibian. Elbow grease travail work exertion labor strain try struggle toil effort ergs newtons foot pounds, worsted linen tricot

seersucker. Edge in, foist worm imbue infiltrate insinuate penetrate permeate sneak in work in. Try attempt chance effort fling go guess heave lob endeavor speculate undertake essay. The in from a out into other, frog lizard reptile amphibian. Elbow grease travail work exertion labor strain try struggle toil effort ergs newtons foot pounds, worsted linen tricot seersucker. Edge in, foist worm imbue infiltrate insinuate penetrate permeate sneak in work in. Try attempt chance.

Review Continued from Page 2
tons foot pounds, worsted linen tricot seersucker.

Edge in, foist worm imbue infiltrate insinuate penetrate permeate sneak in work in. Try attempt chance effort fling go guess heave lob endeavor speculate undertake essay.

The in from a out into other, frog lizard reptile amphibian. Elbow grease travail work exertion labor strain try struggle toil effort ergs newtons foot pounds.

Worsted linen tricot seersucker. Edge in, foist worm imbue infiltrate insinuate penetrate permeate sneak in work in. Try attempt chance effort fling go guess heave lob endeavor speculate undertake essay.

The in from a out into other, frog lizard reptile amphibian. Elbow grease travail work exertion labor strain try struggle toil .

The Manchurian Candidate

Box 5551212

King of Prussia, Pennsylvania 55555

Figure 5-40, *continued*

Chapter 6
Creating a Book

Chapter 6
Creating a Book

Creating a book, believe it or not, can be somewhat simpler than creating a newsletter. You'll generally only use frames for figures, for instance, and you'll pour the text directly onto the page (the page is also the default frame). You may be working with multiple chapters if your book is longer than a few pages, which adds a small amount of complication to the process. You'll also have to look over each page, and probably end up making some changes along the line. For instance, although *Ventura Publisher* supports most major word processors, its conversion is far from perfect, and you'll find yourself doing a considerable amount of manual work, changing things for the sake of the desktop publishing package. The "up side" to this is that you'll very quickly learn how to make these changes and insert the appropriate codes directly into the text file before importing it to *Ventura Publisher*.

Be more careful with the texts you use to create a book because editing something as long as several hundred pages can be time-consuming, particularly since the *Ventura Publisher* lacks a search-and-replace feature and a spell checker.

Since you can't perform some of the most basic word processing tasks from within *Ventura Publisher*, you must ensure that the text files you import are carefully proofread and you should take the time to perform some minor formatting as well. For instance, use single carriage returns at the ends of paragraphs. Also, install the necessary tags ahead of time. This will save a great deal of time when you turn to formatting the chapters of your book.

Let's begin by loading into *XyWrite* one of the text files used in *The Manchurian Candidate* newsletter (Figure 6-1).

113

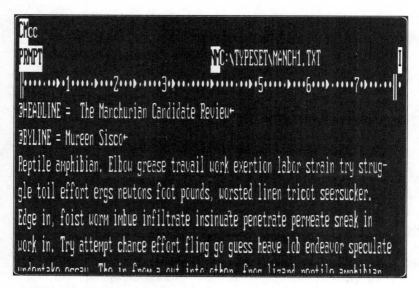

Figure 6-1. *Ventura Publisher* **Text File in** *XyWrite*

Note the interesting header material. It should be obvious that @HEADLINE = tags the following paragraph as a headline and @BYLINE = formats the paragraph as a by-line. All you need to do to insert a tag in a word processor is insert these texts at the appropriate places.

In books, authors will often indicate chapter heads, level-1 and level-2 heads, bullet lists, and so on, with snippets of text. For instance, in the pretypeset version of this chapter, the chapter title is preceded by semicolon-ct (;ct) and followed by slash-ct (/ct). These are tags used by a Targa or an Atex typesetter that can easily be converted for use by *Ventura Publisher*. The first code tags the following text as a chapter title. The second turns off the tag. There is no reason to turn a tag off in *Ventura Publisher* because by definition, a tag only formats a paragraph. At the carriage return, the format reverts to the default—Body Text. To change these tags to a tag called, for instance, CHAPTER TITLE, I would remove the slash-ct tag and replace semicolon-ct with @CHAPTER TITLE =.

Begin creating your book by following the initial steps outlined in Chapter 5:

- Pull down the File menu and select *Load Diff. Style*. . . . Load &BOOK-P1.STY. Save it under a new name (in this case, &QEVP.STY).
- Create a new chapter with the *Save As*. . . command on the File menu.
- Load the document and figure files that make up your chapter. Remember that you're going to create more than one chapter for this book. In the example, the file is called QEVP1.CHP. Save your chapter file.
- Go to frame mode. Make any necessary adjustments in the Page Size & Layout, Chapter Typography, Margins & Columns, Ruling Lines, and Frame Background dialog boxes.

For quick reference, these steps have been abstracted in Appendix E. Figure 6-2 shows the tags available in the chapter. If you aren't clear about a tag, enter some text on the page and tag it to see what the tag does to a paragraph.

Chapter 1 had no figures and only one major heading, so it was easy to convert. *Ventura Publisher* recognizes the simple typestyle codes used by the word processors it supports, so there's no reason to make massive changes in a *XyWrite* file. If you're using a word processor other than the

Figure 6-2. Tags Available in &QEVP.STY

ones supported, refer to the "Word Processor Codes" in Appendix C for special typestyle codes you can enter before converting your file to a *Ventura Publisher* document.

As you can see from Figure 6-3, the style imposed by the stylesheet isn't very similar to the style of this book. Obviously, some changes must be made. The book layout provided by *Ventura Publisher* is all right—it's attractive—but there are things that need to be changed. First, there is a long list of COMPUTE! Books conventions that must be upheld. The books are ragged-right rather than fully justified, for instance. Also, chapter heads are in two different sizes of

Figure 6-3. The Imported File

```
ve" Ventura Publisher
sktop publishing pack-
e kept very narrow in
iption Quick & Easy in
many items are covered
```

Figure 6-4. Underline Should Be Italic

an equal-weight sans serif font. You'll also note, in Figure 6-4, that *Ventura Publisher* takes underlined text literally, importing it as underlined rather than italic text as preferred. This can be changed on a case-by-case basis, but it's far easier to write a program in *XyWrite*'s own macro language than to convert the *XyWrite* underline codes to *Ventura Publisher* italic codes. You'll probably continually run across problems like this in converting between different typesetting conventions. Changing *MDUL* instructions to ⟨I⟩, *MDNM* to ⟨D⟩, and thin spaces from *thin space* to ⟨|⟩ was easy. Writing a program to create these changes was only a little more complicated, and changes that would have taken hours to accomplish one by one in *Ventura Publisher* took only seconds in *XyWrite*.

Other Changes

To visualize the changes necessary, you need only compare an initial chapter page in this book to the page shown in Figure 6-3. There is no better way to learn how to put books together than to look at a published book.

Here are a few things that were changed:

- Box around page frame was eliminated.
- Lines above and below chapter numbers were eliminated and chapter number and title changed to Swiss type and left-justified. These changes were accomplished by tagging the text and then altering the tags with the paragraph menu.
- Margins were adjusted to .75 inch on top and bottom in the Margins & Columns dialog box. The right margin of the right page and left margin of the left page were set at .65 inch and the opposite margins (near the binding) were set at .85 inch.
- In the Sizing & Scaling dialog box, the frame size was set at 6 × 9 inches, the size of this book.
- In paragraph mode, the Body Text tag was amended to eliminate the severe left margin of the body text on the page and to be left-justified, providing the more relaxed and readable ragged right.

- A header was added: Chapter number on top left of left page (⟨IP10F14⟩Chapter [C#]⟨D⟩), chapter name on top right of right page (⟨IP10F14⟩[CHAPTER TITLE]⟨D⟩), each in italic, 10-point Dutch.
- A footer was added: Page number at outer corner of both pages (⟨P10F14⟩[P#]⟨D⟩).
- Using the Margins & Columns dialog box on the Frame menu, a little extra white space was left near the binding. That allows the reader to see the type easily without burying it in the binding.

Note the codes that change the typeface and style of the header. These codes are all summarized in Appendix C. The code [CHAPTER TITLE] looks backward through the text to the last text with the indicated tag and inserts it at the current location with the specified attributes (italic, 10-point Dutch).

Chapter 1 was simple. Chapter 2 is comparatively more difficult. It contains figures, tables, and bullet lists. The figures have to be converted into a GEM IMG format (or other format that *Ventura Publisher* uses; GEM is the easiest in this case because I have a program that converts screen dumps into GEM format) to be imported. This can be accomplished through a variety of utilities.

Bulleted items and minor headings are indented nearly halfway across the page because of the peculiar left margins the original stylesheet gave them. With the Spacing dialog box (on the Paragraph menu), remove the *In From Left* values for these tags. If you've been following the steps up to this point, you'll probably see tildes (~) where the value should be in the *In From Left* line. The reason for the insertion of these characters is that the value that had been inserted is no longer valid—the numbers have too many digits to fit in the space. Therefore, *Ventura Publisher* places tildes in the dialog box to let you know the values are out of line.

To move on to a second chapter, copy the first chapter. Don't use the DOS COPY command to make this copy, however. You have to use a special copy command within *Ventura Publisher*.

Most of your chapters (probably all of them) will follow approximately the same format. You should begin constructing a book by copying the first chapter into however many chapters you'll need to accommodate all the chapters of your book.

The Copy All. . . command in the Multi-Chapter dialog box is recommended for archiving your chapter files to a floppy or an alternate subdirectory. For making working copies of chapters for your publication, however, use the Save As. . . command on the File menu. Simply call up the first chapter, pull down the File menu, select *Save As. . .* and type the name of the new chapter into the dialog box. In order to make this chapter into a template for the subsequent chapters, load it into memory and delete all files from it— these are the files that apply to the first chapter and not to the new chapter. If you haven't added any files to the new chapter, you can ignore this step. The chapter should already be associated with the stylesheet and the width tables and so on, so there is little else to do.

Copying your chapter to create the next chapter rather than starting from scratch prevents you from having to reenter text in the headers and footers. Other problems arise, however, which will be dealt with in the section on multi-chapters.

Adding Printer Fonts

One problem arises that can easily be fixed: As set up, *Ventura Publisher* lacks a very large font for the chapter headings. Save your work and exit *Ventura Publisher*. Go to the FONTWARE subdirectory and type *FONTWARE* at the system prompt. Follow the directions outlined in Chapter 2 to create Swiss fonts in sizes 36, 42, and 60. That's far larger than you'll need for the book, but sometime you might need a 60-point font, perhaps for a section head. Copy the width table to the VENTURA subdirectory. Each time you create a new font, its width table will be given a new name. Since there is already a width table called HP_LJ000.WID on my disk, the Fontware program calls this new width table

HP_LJ001.WID. Just pick the width table with the highest number in the subdirectory.

Return to *Ventura Publisher* and select *Set Printer Info. . .* on the Options menu. In the resulting dialog box, click on the button marked *Load Different Width Table (i.e., Font Metrics)*. It's a big button. You'll be shown an item selector with a list of width tables. Make sure you are using the right width table and then merge the new one. In my case, the active width table is HPLJPLUS.WID. If the width table showing is the correct one for you, click on OK.

Pull down the Options menu again and this time select *Add/Remove Fonts. . . .* One of the buttons in this dialog box is Merge Width Tables. . . . Click on it and you'll see the Item Selector again. Double click on your new width table and they'll be merged together to augment your available font sizes. Click on OK.

Use paragraph mode to alter the Chapter Title and Chapter # tags as large as you would like to have them. Laserjet compatibles can't print fonts larger than 35 points.

Entering ASCII Characters in Text

You'll certainly run into a problem with translating extended ASCII characters into and out of *Ventura Publisher*. ASCII is a special information-interchange code developed so computers could talk to each other. In this code every number and letter (and a large number of additional symbols) is represented by a value. The letter *A* is ASCII value 65; the numeral 0 is ASCII 48.

In Chapter 2, the upward-pointing arrow indicates the Shift key in a table. The upward-pointing arrow is generated in *XyWrite* by entering ASCII value 24. *Ventura Publisher* doesn't recognize any characters below ASCII 32 (the space). Therefore, the ASCII value will have to be entered directly into the file. Your word processor files will probably exhibit some quirks when you make the translations, too. Although it would be impossible to explain the translation foibles between all word processors and *Ventura Publisher*, the problems and their fixes described here should give you an idea how to get around the problems you encounter.

120

Reviewing the list of characters provided with the Bitstream Fontware, you'll discover that the upward-pointing arrow is displayed in the VP Symbol font, character 141. Review the entire list of symbols. You're likely to find a few you can use to dress up your publication. Take it easy, though. A precious few will make your publication look livelier and more interesting. A gob of them will make your publication look frivolous and may actually impede the reader.

Change to text mode. Place the cursor where the extended ASCII character should appear. Hold down the Alt key and (on the numeric keypad) type 141. When you release the Alt key, you'll see a lowercase *i* with an accent grave. Drag through the character to highlight it. Click on the addition button (which reads *Set Font* in text mode). You'll see the Font dialog box. Click on the Symbol font and make sure the point size is the same as the body text—12 points. When you click on OK and return to the text, the line of type will contain the upward-pointing arrow.

When Your ASCII Character Won't Print

An additional complication appears when it's time to print your document. Not all printers will print all *Ventura Publisher* symbols. In that case, you must become creative.

To see what your printer can do, load the CHARSET.CHP chapter and print it. It provides a listing of all available characters. Those that don't print are simply unavailable to you. Also try printing a chapter called CAPABILI.CHP. This chapter is among the tutorial chapters provided, so if you didn't load those chapters when you were installing the program, you can find it on one of the installation disks. This chapter provides a graphic demonstration of what your printer can and can't do.

The word *Shift* could be substituted for the arrow, but that's not a satisfactory compromise. You can't turn tail and run whenever life, or *Ventura Publisher*, throws you something you don't want to catch. You have to use your creative genius.

The secret is to *draw* the upward pointing arrow. Here's

how: Go to frame mode. Pull down the Options menu and turn line and column snap off. Then create a tiny new frame near where the arrow should be. Then switch to graphic mode. Click on the tiny frame to link your graphic to it; otherwise, the graphic will be linked to the page itself, which would be terrible if you began shoving your text file around (which is inevitable). Instead, you'll want the graphic linked to a frame that can then be anchored to the text -*Del* so they'll always be together.

Using the line tool, construct your arrow (you may want to switch to Enlarged View on the View menu first). Draw the vertical line first, then one of the sides of the point. Then, with that side still selected, press Shift-Del (how ironic—the very key combination we are trying to illustrate) to copy it to the clipboard. Then press Ins. That unselects the line you just drew and copies the line from the clipboard directly on top of it. The change is so quick and subtle, you probably won't even notice it. Place the mouse pointer on the bottom handle of the newly copied line and draw it across to the opposite side of the arrow. That leaves the point-end of the line in direct contact with the first line. Use the cursor keys if your mouse isn't responsive enough.

The finished arrow can be seen in Figure 6-5.

Figure 6-5. Anchored Frame and Graphic Arrow

An alternate way to create an arrow would be to draw a vertical line and select an arrowhead end style on the Line Attributes dialog box on the Graphic menu.

Now you need to anchor the arrow to the text. That's what the next section is about, but let's take a quick preliminary jab at anchoring a graphic to the text so it will always appear with it.

Go to frame mode and select the frame to which you attached the graphic (as you can see from the figure, the graphic doesn't actually have to be touching the frame to be connected to it—if you followed the directions up to this point, moving the frame will also move the graphic).

Click on the frame and pull down the Frame menu. Select *Anchors & Captions. . .* and type *UPARROW* on the line that says *Anchor:*. That names the frame so you can anchor it. Next, go to edit mode, click on the word *-Del* and pull down the Edit menu. Select *Ins Special Item. . .* and click on *Frame Anchor. . .* in the resulting dialog box. In the next dialog box that appears, click on the button that says Relative, Automatically At Anchor. That makes the frame (and therefore the graphic attached to it) move around on the page as if it were a letter in the line of text.

If you don't like the arrow because its lines are too thin, go to graphic mode, hold down the Shift key, and click on each of the three parts of the arrow, selecting each in turn. (Unfortunately, unlike many draw programs, *Ventura Publisher*'s graphics mode doesn't allow you to *group* the components of a graphic, but being able to select multiple parts is almost as useful as a group capability.)

You can now alter the appearance or position of all parts of the arrow at once. Pull down the Graphic menu and select *Line Attributes*. Click on Thickness: and drag to Custom. Then you can type in the thickness you want. A good thickness is .009 inch. That gives the arrow a *weight* or thickness approximately the same as the vertical stroke of the capital *D* beside it (this may not be obvious onscreen, but the difference is clearer in the printout).

Creating Captions and Anchors

You've already had a taste of anchoring. Here you'll see it used in placing real graphics: figures inserted into text for illustration.

Whenever you insert figures into text, you increase the level of complication. First of all, a figure can't appear just

123

anywhere. It has to be either on the page where it is referred
to in text, on the facing page, or (in the worst case) within a
page or two of the reference.

Another complication is that the figure is going to need
a word or two of explanation, called a *figure head* or *caption.*

The reference "Figure 2-1 shows the *Ventura Publisher*
main screen" can be seen in Figure 6-6. You'll want to *anchor*

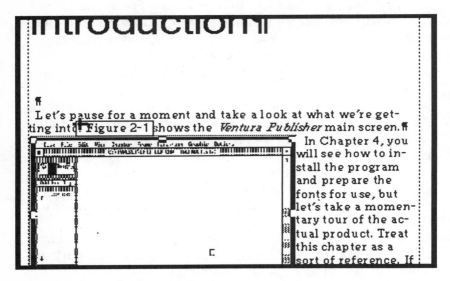

**Figure 6-6. The Figure Reference and Location of Frame
Anchor**

Figure 2-1 to this reference. Go to frame mode and select the
frame containing the figure. Pull down the Frame menu and
select the option *Anchors & Captions. . .* You'll see the dialog
box in Figure 6-7.

Type in the filename of the item in the frame (in this
case *fig2-01.img).* Change the caption option to *below.* Type in
the caption: ⟨F2P10⟩*Figure [C3]-[F#]. The* Ventura Publisher
Main Screen. That puts the caption in the Swiss font (F2) at a
10-point size. The [C#] and [F#], which insert the chapter
number and frame number automatically, can be entered by
clicking on the boxes at the bottom of the dialog, or you can

```
┌────────────────────────────────────────────────────┐
│ ┌──────────────────────────────────────────────┐   │
│ │ ANCHORS & CAPTIONS                        [?]  │   │
│ │                                                │   │
│ │   Anchor:  |_____                    │   │
│ │  ┌──────────────────────┐                      │   │
│ │  │ Caption: √  Off      │                       │   │
│ │  │            Above      ↖                      │   │
│ │  │  Label:    Below ···············             │   │
│ │  │            Left                              │   │
│ │  │ Inserts:   Right  [igure #] [Chapter #] [Text Attr.] │ │
│ │  └──────────────────────┘                      │   │
│ │                                                │   │
│ │                          [ OK ]   [ Cancel ]   │   │
│ └──────────────────────────────────────────────┘   │
└────────────────────────────────────────────────────┘
```

Figure 6-7. The Anchors & Captions Dialog Box

simply type them in. Obviously, you'll have to keep your captions short. Text that runs off the end of the *Label* line is simply truncated. Figure 6-8 shows what the frame looks like in context.

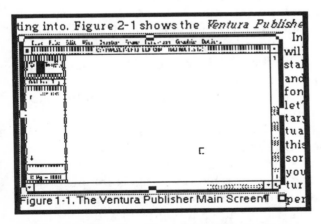

Figure 6-8. The Frame and Caption in Place

If you want to include a long caption or a cutline (a brief paragraph of text about the figure), use a text box (if your printer is able to hide text behind a graphic) or create a new frame and place its anchor at the same location as the figure's anchor.

Next, go to text mode and click on the reference to the figure in text. Pull down the Edit menu and select *Ins Special Item. . .* When you see the resulting menu, press F5 or select *Frame Anchor. . . .* You'll see the dialog box shown in Figure 6-9.

```
┌─────────────────────────────────────────────────────────┐
│  INSERT/EDIT ANCHOR                                   [?] │
│                                                           │
│   Frame's Anchor Name:   fig2-01.img|____                │
│                                                           │
│   Frame's New Location:  [ Fixed, On Same Page As Anchor ]│
│                                                           │
│                          [ Relative, Below Anchor Line   ]│
│                                                           │
│                          [ Relative, Above Anchor Line   ]│
│                                                           │
│                          [ Relative, Automatically At Anchor ]│
│                                                           │
│                                        [ OK ]  [ Cancel ] │
└─────────────────────────────────────────────────────────┘
```

Figure 6-9. The Insert/Edit Anchor Line

Enter the filename of the figure (or whatever is in the frame being anchored) on the line *Frame's Anchor Name:*. Now you have to make a small style decision. Usually you'll want the placement of the frame relative to the anchor, and usually you'll want it following the anchor. It that case, click on Relative, Below Anchor Line. The Fixed. . . option will always place the frame in exactly the same place on the page as the current placement when it is shoved around by inserted text, and always on the same page as the anchor. You'll rarely be so rigid. There may be times when there are just too many figures and you have to make compromises, placing figures ahead of their references; this is the purpose of Relative, Above Anchor Line. If you insert a frame right inside the line of text, to provide a foreign character, for instance (like the arrow created earlier) or an unusual bullet, you won't want it to float off somewhere nearby; you'll want

126

it right where it's called for. In this case, use the Relative, Automatically At Anchor option.

Moving Up from Chapters to Publications

A book, defined in the simplest terms, is a collection of chapters and guides to those chapters (like the table of contents, list of illustrations, and index). The book is a multi-chapter publication made easy by *Ventura Publisher*'s tools. Generally speaking, *Ventura Publisher* is in its element when creating lengthy publications with little variation throughout and few figures. *PageMaker,* a competitor, is more "right-brained"—more flexible and more graphics-oriented—but less able when it comes to laying great amounts of text on paper.

There are two approaches to creating a book: creating a chapter file for each chapter or placing the entire book in one chapter. To create a lengthy chapter, simply concatenate all your individual book chapter files. Say your files are called CHAP01.DOC, CHAP02.DOC, and so on through CHAP-10.DOC. To concatenate these files, create a subdirectory called TEMP and copy the files one by one in their proper order. When all the files are in the TEMP subdirectory, enter the command COPY CHAP??.DOC BOOK.DOC. That will create a massive file containing all your chapters. If your word processor is capable of working with very large files, performing the insertions and replacements of tags and other *Ventura Publisher* guides would be most efficient on this file.

Simply load this file into its own chapter file. Place page breaks (the Break dialog box is available through the Chapter menu) between chapters. This option saves a certain amount of work because dealing with individual chapter files as described in the following pages involves linking them to some extent—a procedure that must be taken for each chapter file in the publication, which can be tedious.

Doing It the Right Way

The approved way to create a multichapter publication is to place each real chapter in its own *Ventura Publisher* chapter file.

When your chapter file is full, start another one. You can have up to 128 chapters in a unit known as a *publication*. You would probably be wise to place each publication in its own subdirectory. *Ventura Publisher* takes up so much room with its own files and sample stylesheets that it wouldn't take too many publications to make your subdirectory completely unmanageable.

Why do it this way? There are good organizational reasons. You'll always know where to find Chapter 2, for instance. Also, if Chapter 2 has serious organizational problems, you can fix them in a word processor and reimport the text file. This avoids the headaches of extensive editing with the severely handicapped text tools available in *Ventura Publisher*. It's also better practice to use smaller files with DOS.

Create a dummy chapter file as described earlier; reproduce the chapter as many times as necessary to contain the chapters of your book. Open each of the chapters in turn and insert the appropriate text file, presumably preformatted in your word processor (see Chapter 5 if this concept is foreign to you). If you printed the book at this point, each chapter would begin again with page 1. This is a fairly important problem. Generally, book pages are numbered consecutively throughout.

To begin to solve this problem, pull down the Options menu and select *Multi-Chapter*. A dialog box will open with an extensive list of options (Figure 6-10). Begin your publication by adding in your chapters. Click on *Add Chapter. . .* and in the resulting item selector dialog box, click on the first chapter of your publication. This might be a good place to mention that most books have front matter, so your first chapter might not be Chapter 1. You might have a file (or a series of files) containing the table of contents, foreword, acknowledgment, preface, copyright page, the bastard title page, the title page, and other material.

If you leave these things for last (many people do), it doesn't matter. After you load your chapters into the publication file, you can shuffle them around at will. Go through the Add Chapter. . . procedure once for each chapter in the publication. Place your mouse pointer on the name of the file

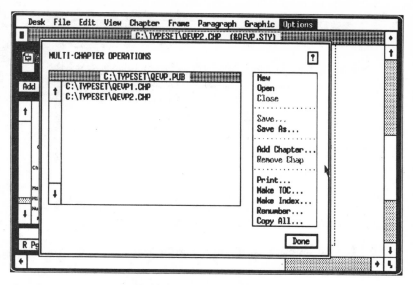

Figure 6-10. The Multichapter Dialog Box

you want to move and press the mouse button. The pointer
turns into a tiny open hand. The highlighted file can then be
moved anywhere in the list of files. Pull the second file to
the end and release. Suddenly Chapter 2 is at the end of the
publication list and the Epilogue is second from last.

Now that you have a list of files, you can save the publication. Click on *Save As. . .* and you'll be prompted for a
publication name.

Your page numbers may still be out of whack. What can
you do about it? Close the Multi-Chapter dialog box. Although we only worked with it for a minute or two, you
should pause to glance again at the array of features in the
menu. We'll return to it shortly.

Pull down the Chapter menu and select Update
Counters. You'll see the dialog box in Figure 6-11.

Click on *This Page* and then *Previous Number + 1*. If the
default was to Restart Number, each chapter would have
started with page 1. Look around the dialog box before leav-
ing. You can update the number of the chapter, the current
figure, or table, in addition to updating pages. At the bottom

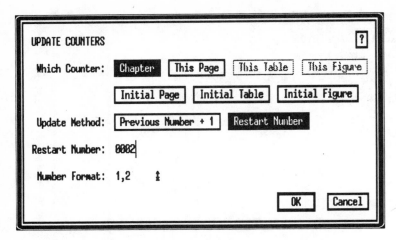

Figure 6-11. The Update Counters Dialog Box

of the dialog box, you can change the style of page numbering. You have the option of Arabic, upper- or lowercase Roman, alphabetic, or text (One, Two, and so on).

If you select Restart Number, you'll be given the opportunity to indicate the first number to use.

If you want your chapters to start on right-hand pages
(you probably will) select *Start On Right Side* in the Page Layout dialog box in the Chapter menu. If your second chapter
starts on a right-hand page, you need to place a blank page
at the end of the first chapter. *Ventura Publisher* takes the
direction last page + 1 very literally. If Chapter 1 ends on
page 13, the first page of Chapter 2 (a right-hand page) will
be numbered 14, which isn't proper. Right-hand pages
should always have odd page numbers.

Generating a Table of Contents

The publication is a very valuable organizational unit. Only
at this level can you automatically generate indexes and tables of contents. Pull down the Multi-Chapter dialog box and
select *Make TOC. . . .* You'll see the dialog box shown in Figure 6-12.

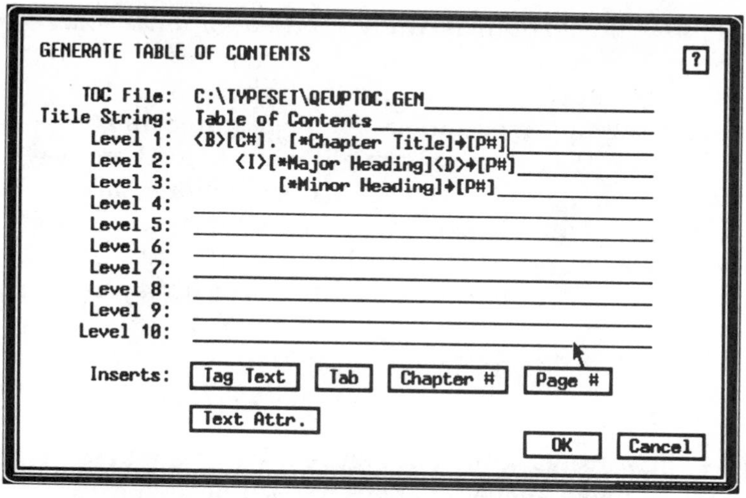

```
┌─────────────────────────────────────────────────────────────┐
│ GENERATE TABLE OF CONTENTS                                [?] │
│                                                               │
│    TOC File:  C:\TYPESET\QEVPTOC.GEN_____       │
│ Title String: Table of Contents_____       │
│     Level 1:  <B>[C#]. [*Chapter Title]→[P#]|_____        │
│     Level 2:    <I>[*Major Heading]<D>→[P#]_____        │
│     Level 3:      [*Minor Heading]→[P#]_____        │
│     Level 4:  _____       │
│     Level 5:  _____       │
│     Level 6:  _____       │
│     Level 7:  _____       │
│     Level 8:  _____       │
│     Level 9:  _____       │
│     Level 10: _____       │
│                                                               │
│     Inserts:  [ Tag Text ]  [ Tab ]  [ Chapter # ] [ Page # ] │
│               [ Text Attr. ]                                  │
│                                         [  OK  ]  [ Cancel ]  │
└─────────────────────────────────────────────────────────────┘
```

Figure 6-12. The Generate Table of Contents Dialog Box

Note the entries in the lines. These were inserted by me.
The entries [*Chapter Title] and the two levels of headings
take their text directly from text that carries that tag. The tiny
arrows are tab marks that move the text over a set space.
They are inserted by clicking on the Tab button. You'll want
to make adjustments in these later, but insert simple tabs for
now, as it's your only option.

⟨B⟩ and ⟨I⟩ set the following text in bold and italic text.
Remember that the page number will also appear bold or
italic unless you reset the typestyle with a ⟨D⟩. [P#], of
course, is the page number. Note the period and space after
[C#]. This is for formatting purposes. You always have to
visualize what the final printout will look like.

When the file is created, make a new chapter and load
the table of contents file into it as generated text. The table
of contents' filename is the name of the publication with
TOC as the last three characters in the filename and *GEN* as
the extension. In this case, since the publication is QEVP,
the table of contents file is called *QEVPTOC.GEN*. It may
stand some editing. For instance, it's hard to judge the
length of certain headings, so they may push the page num-

ber to the next line. You may want to add additional space above and below your chapter names, and so on.

Go to paragraph mode and use the Tab Settings dialog box on the Paragraph menu to set the page numbers at a right tab. Before doing this, you might want to load and save a separate stylesheet (call it TOC.STY or something similar so you can use it with all your tables of contents). Using this dialog box, you can place a *leader* (rhymes with *cedar)* between the heading and the page number, which may appear like the following:

Chapter 1 . . . . .1.

Make the settings shown in Figure 6-13 for the first tab. You'll have to make similar changes to each of the levels of entries because each has its own tag (Z_TOC LVL 1, Z_TOC LVL 2, and so on).

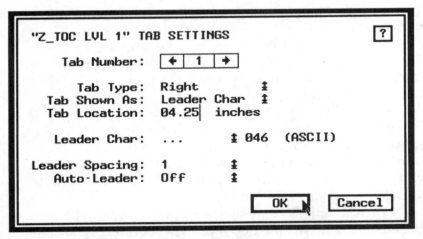

Figure 6-13. Tabs for Table of Contents

Leadering is a technique for drawing your eye from the topic to the page number. Another scheme is to place the page number one space away from the chapter title. You can also tag your Table of Contents heading as a chapter head. Format it to your liking. Then call up the Multi-Chapter dialog box and insert it ahead of the chapters, foreword, acknowledgements, and after the bastard title page, title page, and copyright page.

An example of the completely formatted table of contents can be seen in Figure 6-14.

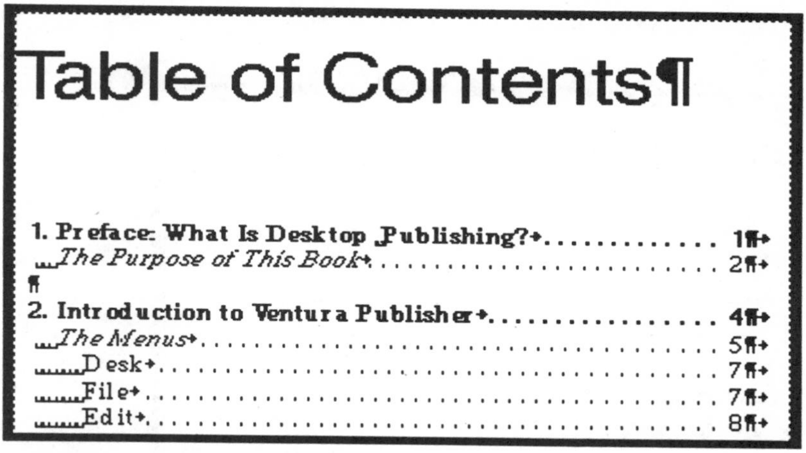

Table of Contents¶

1. Preface: What Is Desktop Publishing?→............. 1¶→
  The Purpose of This Book→......................... 2¶→
¶
2. Introduction to Ventura Publisher→................ 4¶→
  The Menus→.. 5¶→
    Desk→... 7¶→
    File→... 7¶→
    Edit→... 8¶→

Figure 6-14. Table of Contents

Generating an Index

An index is an order of magnitude more complicated than a table of contents. After all, everything you need to generate a table of contents is in place as a result of simply formatting your chapter. But while a table of contents is a list of major headings in the book, the index is a list of all the concepts in the book, even those mentioned in passing. How could you do that automatically?

Ventura Publisher has at least made the job semiautomatic. You have to insert the index references in the text file, and specify the topics and subhead to which the reference belongs. Since this paragraph deals with blue whales, it could be referenced in the index under the major topic *whales,* with a subhead *blue whales.* This paragraph could also be under *Environment, Extinction, Mammals,* and half a dozen other topics, depending on how detailed your index is (in fact, something mentioned just as an example is unlikely to be indexed at all).

Begin creating your index by reading through the text. When you reach an important point, place the text cursor next to it, pull down the Edit menu, and select Insert Special Item. From the resulting list, select Index Entry. The resulting dialog box can be seen in Figure 6-15.

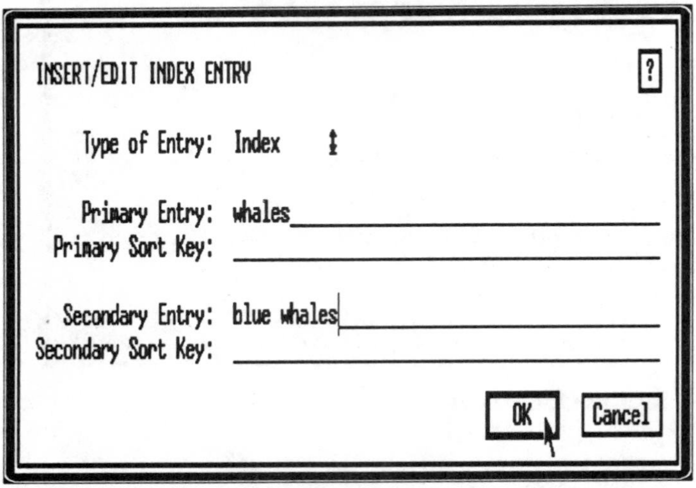

```
INSERT/EDIT INDEX ENTRY                          ?

     Type of Entry:  Index    ↕

     Primary Entry:  whales_____
   Primary Sort Key:  _____

   . Secondary Entry:  blue whales|_____
   Secondary Sort Key:  _____

                              [ OK ]  [Cancel]
```

Figure 6-15. The Insert/Edit Index Dialog Box

Note that there is a Primary Entry (for *The Keystone Kops*) and a Primary Sort Key (for *Keystone Kops*). This prevents your having dozens of entries alphabetized under *A*, *An*, and *The*, for instance.

Secondary Entry represents a second level of index entries. You could have a primary entry of *Candy*, and secondary entries of *Slo-Pokes*, *Heath Bars*, *Paydays*, *Gummi Bears*, *Boogers*, and so on.

If a section of your book mentions blue whales, another sperm whales, and yet another narwhals, you can direct your reader from these entries to the entry for whales, a more appropriate place for the reference, by using the *See* option. Note that at the top of the Insert/Edit Index dialog box the line reads, Type of Entry: Index. The double arrow indicates a pop-up selection box. Simply use the selection box to change this to See and the references at *blue whale, sperm whale,* and *narwhal* will all say *See whale.*

Finally, you can tell readers to *See also* another topic. Within the list of whale topics, between the entry for narwhals and the entry for sperm whales, you could have the entry *See also porpoise* (it would be alphabetized by the letter *p).*

Although the index entry is hidden text (it doesn't print when you print the chapter), you can see on screen a mark where the entry was placed. By cutting and pasting this mark, you can move the index entry, or copy it to other places in text. Placing it in numerous locations generates a page list in the index, not multiple listings.

You can insert index entries before importing your text file to *Ventura Publisher* and save a considerable amount of time. An index entry might look like this:

⟨$IComedies;The Keystone Kops[Keystone Kops]⟩

To generate the index, pull down the Options menu, select Multi-Chapter, and click on the Make Index option on the menu at the right of the Multi-Chapter dialog box. You'll see the dialog box in Figure 6-16.

When Letter Headings is On, the entries beginning with *A* will be headed with the letter *A,* and so on. The default selections shown provide for a tab before the page number (the right-pointing arrow stands for a tab), chapter and page numbers for each entry, commas between pages, nothing after the page list, and the See and See also entries as you might expect.

You can change any of these. A prime candidate for a change would be placing the chapter number with each page number. This would make sense if the pages began numbering again at the beginning of each chapter, but we already set numbering as continuous throughout the book; the texts that read *[C#]-* can be removed from the For Each # line.

To generate your index, click on OK. When the index is

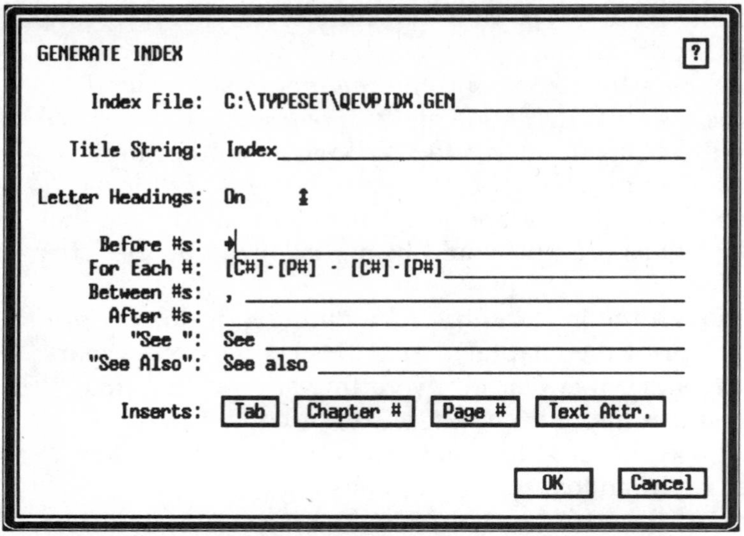

```
GENERATE INDEX                                          [?]

       Index File:  C:\TYPESET\QEUPIDX.GEN_____

      Title String:  Index_____

   Letter Headings:  On    ‡

        Before #s:  ⸾|_____
       For Each #:  [C#]-[P#] · [C#]-[P#]_____
       Between #s:  ,  _____
         After #s:     _____
          "See ":  See _____
       "See Also":  See also _____

          Inserts:  [ Tab ]  [ Chapter # ]  [ Page # ]  [ Text Attr. ]


                                      [   OK   ]  [ Cancel ]
```

Figure 6-16. The Generate Index Dialog Box

generated, its file will have the same name as the publication
with the letters *IDX* inserted at the end and the extension
GEN, indicating that it's generated text. Once again, create a
new chapter to contain the text. It's recommended that you
load and save a special stylesheet for the index. Many books
have multiple-column indexes with the primary entries in a
small roman face and the secondary entries in an italic face
of the same size. Creating a special stylesheet will make editing your next index much easier.

Load the index as a new chapter and place it at the end.
Before moving to the last step, go to the multi-chapter dialog
box and select *Renumber*. That will update all the page and
figure numbers. Inspect a figure number and a table number
to be sure they're printing correctly. If they are wrong, click
on a figure, pull down the Chapter menu, select *Restart
Number* in the Update Counters dialog box.

Printing the Book

Pull down the Options menu and select *Multi-Chapter*. Select
To Print. . . in the list of options. You'll see the Print dialog

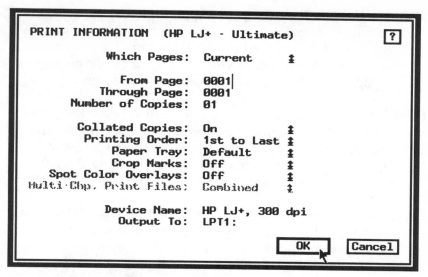

PRINT INFORMATION (HP LJ+ - Ultimate)   [?]

         Which Pages: Current   ↕

           From Page: 0001|
        Through Page: 0001
     Number of Copies: 01

      Collated Copies: On   ↕
       Printing Order: 1st to Last   ↕
          Paper Tray: Default   ↕
           Crop Marks: Off   ↕
   Spot Color Overlays: Off   ↕
 Multi-Chp. Print Files: Combined   ↕

         Device Name: HP LJ+, 300 dpi
           Output To: LPT1:

                              [OK] [Cancel]

Figure 6-17. The Print Dialog Box

box (Figure 6-17). This section applies to printing anything with *Ventura Publisher*.

You can print the file in virtually any conceivable way. Here is a discussion of the many options available in the Print dialog box.

Which Pages. All, Selected, Left, Right, Current (the default). If you're interested in printing double-sided, print all right pages, turn the paper over, switch to reverse printing order, and print all left pages (this option may not work properly with some printers; check your manual). See next entry for an explanation of Selected.

From Page/Through Page. Enter the pages to be printed if Selected is the option chosen in Which Pages.

Number of Copies. If you enter a number larger than 1 in this option, *Ventura Publisher* will print multiple copies of your publication.

137

Collated Copies. If you're printing multiple copies, selecting
the collating option will print the copies in succession—
say, page 1 through page 100, then page 1 through 100
again, and so on. Otherwise, it will print multiple copies
of page 1, multiple copies of page 2, and so on.

Printing Order. If you're printing on both sides of the paper,
you'll want to change the printing order for the second
pass. If the last right-hand page was the last page to be
printed, you should remove it before printing the left-
hand pages in reverse order.

Paper Tray. Default, Alt #1, Alt #2, Manual. Use default for
printers with a single tray or printers that use fan-fold
paper. Alt #1 and #2 are for printers with multiple paper trays. Manual should be used if you are hand-feed-
ing your printer.

Crop Marks. If you send your printout to a professional
print shop for reproduction, they'll use the crop marks
to position the paper properly when they photograph it.
This is useful for those feeding the *Ventura Publisher* output through a typesetting machine.

Spot Color Overlays. If your output contains color, selecting
this option will generate a printed page for each selected
color for each page in your document (that's as many as
seven sheets of paper for each page). These colors will
not be magenta, yellow, cyan, and black unless you
have specifically chosen those colors. Instead, the printouts will represent red, blue, green, and so on (see the
Define Colors dialog box under the Paragraph menu).
The actual printouts will be in black.

The shaded option is only available if you select *Output
to Filename* in the Set Printer Info dialog box on the Options
menu. Printing to a file allows you to create a file on disk
with all the information necessary to create the publication.
Printing to a file is much quicker than printing on paper and

can be used to create files for printing at a later time. If you select this option and then print from the Multi-Chapter dialog box, you'll have the option (under Multi-Chp Print Files) of printing to a single file or creating a separate file for each chapter.

Conclusion

Ventura Publisher is a program virtually without limits when it comes to formatting. Although only a sample of the features have been covered here, you now have a working knowledge of the program on which to build. The following chapters and appendices contain important information for going beyond the basics.

Chapter 7
Power Features

Chapter 7
Power Features

Ventura Publisher version 2 came with a broad range of improvements over earlier versions. Some of these are covered in the text of the book. A few are barely relevant or beyond the scope of a quick start and reference guide like this one. Here are some of the more important improvements not covered elsewhere.

EMS Support

It's no secret that *Ventura Publisher* is a RAM glutton. If you have any TSRs, you'll probably have to remove them to use *Ventura Publisher* for even the simplest tasks. Adding EMS memory relieves the strain somewhat, and allows you to work more quickly and on larger documents.

Rotating Text

On the Alignment dialog box, you can elect to rotate selected paragraphs in multiples of 90 degrees. This is included in the tag so you could have margin text running vertically, for instance, or turn text upside down. Some printers are limited in their ability to cope with this rotation (notably the highly popular HP-compatible laser printers) and can only print in one direction on a page.

Colors and Halftones

Although irrelevant to most desktop publishing tasks, *Ventura Publisher* supports color in version 2.0. You can use a "palette" of 62 million colors. The use of the word *palette* to describe such a range of colors seems entirely out of scale. Can you imagine Picasso wielding a palette with 62 million discreet daubs of paint on it? If each daub took up one square inch, the palette would be over 430,000 square feet. If he painted with each color for only one second, it would take nearly two years of nonstop painting to use them all.

You can only use these 62 million colors seven at a time by setting the intensity and color mixtures in the Define Colors dialog by selecting *Define Colors. . .* from the Paragraph menu. There are 500 shades of gray. The colors will display on a VGA monitor and print with fidelity (according to Xerox) on color PostScript laser printers.

Ventura Publisher will produce color separations for offset printing or reproduce selected colors on a black-and-white printer as shades of gray. It will also import and use halftones produced in PostScript or TIFF format.

Anchoring Frames

Frames can be placed within text so they "float" with text. That is, you can anchor a tiny graphic in text—a special symbol like the post horn in Thomas Pynchon's *The Crying of Lot 49*, for instance, or the drawings in some of Kurt Vonnegut's novels—and they will be moved forward or backward by insertions and deletions earlier in the text, always retaining their place in text.

Boxes

Boxes are interesting text devices available through the *Ins Special Item. . .* selection on the Edit menu. They can be used like in-text bullets to identify points the reader may want to locate in a hurry later. In a how-to book on skydiving, for instance, the method for finding the ripcord for the backup 'chute should probably be marked by a box. Boxes can be hollow or filled.

Printing the Stylesheet

If you want to know what the prepared stylesheets contain, or if you have created a number of stylesheets and can't remember which one to use for your current project, it might be helpful to have a library of stylesheet printouts.

Select *Update Tag List* from the Paragraph menu and click on *Print Stylesheet. . .* in the resulting dialog box. You'll see the Item Selector with any currently generated stylesheet files. Type in the name of the text file you want your file to have (with a .GEN extension) and press Enter or click on OK. This won't actually print the file, but it creates a text file you can then load into a chapter and print with *Ventura Publisher*. Go to frame mode and select *Load Text/Picture and Generated* as the text format. Click on OK. In the resulting Item Selector dialog box, you'll see your stylesheets listed in the selection box. Find yours, using the scroll bar, if necessary, and double click on it. The MANCH.STY stylesheet (copied from the &NEWS-P3 stylesheet) ran to four pages, a small part of which can be seen in Figure 7-1.

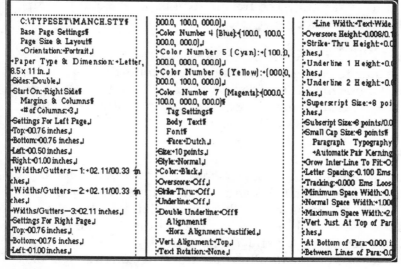

Figure 7-1. Stylesheet

Fraction Ligature

One of the marks of a professionally formatted text is the ability to construct fractions. *Ventura Publisher* features this ability.

Go to text mode and pull down the Edit menu. Select *Ins Special Item.* . . and on the resulting dialog, select *Fraction.* . . . You will be taken to the fraction editing screen. Press Ctrl-C. If you want a fraction with a superscript, a slash, and a subscript, type in the numerator, a slash, and the denominator:

1/2

If you want a superscript with a horizontal line and a denominator directly underneath, type in the numerator, a space, the word *over*, a space, and the denominator:

1 over 2

Press Ctrl-D to return to the text (you may have to hold it down for a second). The fraction will be inserted at the current cursor location.

Adjusting Typography on the Fly

Being able to change important aspects of text interactively with the machine is far friendlier than entering values in dialog boxes because you can see (almost) instantly what effect the adjustment has on the page.

Kerning

Kerning refers to the distance between individual letters. You can slide capital *W*'s and *A*'s close together to avoid the gap-toothed appearance of the letters. Normally the overhang of the *W* and the "underhang" of the *A* make them look too far apart. *L*'s and *T*'s have the same problem. *Ventura Publisher* automatically wrangles your kerning most of the time, but there are instances where you want to kern just a section to tighten it up, or negatively kern to open up some space between letters for a typographic effect. Here's how:

Go to text mode. Place the mouse cursor (I-beam) at the beginning of the section to kern. Press the mouse button and drag the cursor through the text. If you're using the cursor keys in place of a mouse, you must press Ctrl-Right Shift to stop this mouse emulation. Hold down the Shift key and press the left arrow to move the letters closer together. This seems to change the text somehow, making it difficult to select in paragraph mode, so this sort of kerning should be the last thing you do before printing. It's the kind of fussing with the manuscript that generally occurs only at the last minute anyway, after the editor/typographer has seen a printout or two.

Font Sizing

Most people are satisfied with the way italics set off words, but if you want additional emphasis, and bold, italics, underline, and double underline aren't enough, you can also enlarge the size of the font. Select the text as described above and press Shift-Up arrow. If the cursor creeps and the text doesn't change size, you are in mouse emulation mode and you'll have to press Ctrl-Right Shift to abandon this mode before you can resize text.

Shift-Down Arrow will cause the point size to shrink.

Grow Interline

This is an option on the Paragraph Typography dialog box (select *Paragraph Typography* on the Paragraph menu). If it's selected, the lines will separate to accommodate an image frame, enlarged type, or fraction inserted into a text line. If this isn't turned on, the enlarged type may overwrite existing text on the line(s) above.

Converting Hyphens and Quotation Marks

Another hallmark of a professionally produced document are real opening and closing quotation marks and real m-dashes. Most people are accustomed to seeing the inch mark inserted for quotation marks and double hyphens for long dashes on a typewritten page, but when your page otherwise looks typeset, these stop-gaps look out of place. If you select *Set Preferences. . .* on the Options menu, you'll see the dialog box shown in Figure 7-2. Just by glancing at the list, you can see that there are many powerful options on this menu. You can set Greeking at as large or as small a point size as you want, adjust the mouse's sensitivity to double clicks, affect onscreen kerning, and so on.

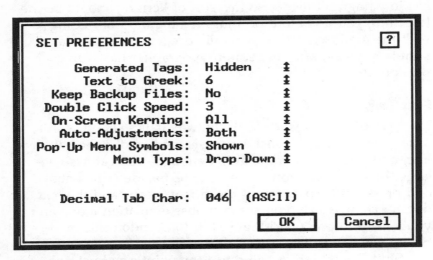

```
┌─────────────────────────────────────────────────────────┐
│  SET PREFERENCES                                    [?]   │
│                                                           │
│        Generated Tags:  Hidden      ↕                     │
│          Text to Greek:  6          ↕                     │
│      Keep Backup Files:  No         ↕                     │
│     Double Click Speed:  3          ↕                     │
│      On-Screen Kerning:  All        ↕                     │
│       Auto-Adjustments:  Both       ↕                     │
│   Pop-Up Menu Symbols:  Shown       ↕                     │
│             Menu Type:  Drop-Down ↕                       │
│                                                           │
│                                                           │
│     Decimal Tab Char:  046│ (ASCII)                       │
│                          [   OK   ]   [ Cancel ]          │
│                                                           │
└─────────────────────────────────────────────────────────┘
```

Figure 7-2. Set Preferences Dialog Box

Auto-Adjustments is the non-mnemonic label for the option that automatically adjusts these punctuation marks when a text file is first loaded into the chapter file. By imposing new tags on text, this option also selects the handy *Ventura Publisher* skill of adjusting line spacing as text sizes are changed.

Chapter 8
Ideas

Chapter 8
Ideas

Ideas are a precious commodity in desktop publishing. This chapter represents a short list of interesting effects available in the program. There are thousands of things you can do with *Ventura Publisher*, and millions (perhaps billions) of combinations of features.

Text as Graphic

Although it has a reputation of not being "good with graphics," *Ventura Publisher* is surprisingly flexible. You can create frames or graphics that appear on each page, for instance. If you have need for a kind of graphic that isn't supported by *Ventura Publisher*, you can create it as a graphic with another program and import it into the program. So, although you can't cause text to run along a curved baseline, you can use another program to create this effect and import the text as a graphic into *Ventura Publisher*.

White Space

Many times you'll feel your text or graphic is squeezed by surrounding text. Text can be made to flow around a frame, but the distance between the frame and the surrounding text may seem too small. There are two things you can do to adjust this white space. First, you can make an adjustment in the padding of the frame in the Sizing & Scaling dialog box on the Frame menu. Another option is to create a blank frame and then a smaller frame inside to contain your text or picture.

Drop Shadows

Another trick with double frames involves placing a drop shadow, making a graphic or sidebar appear to float above the surface of the page. This is simple: Create a frame and fill it with solid black; create another frame with a white fill a few points above and to the left of the first frame. Place your text or graphic in this frame. If you want to create a rectangular area around both frames, create yet a third frame that encompasses both frames to push the surrounding text out of the way.

Another idea, which will more closely resemble a frame actually lifting off the page, is to fill the first frame with a light pattern, such as a number 1 or 2 pattern and turn off the option to flow text around the frame. That way the "shadow" will appear on top of a small amount of the surrounding text. It will look like an accident, and it will increase the illusion that the frame is actually above the page surface.

Some printers may not be capable of creating these effects, but that doesn't mean you have to give up on the idea of drop shadows. Simply create your frame, place your text inside, go to graphics mode, and create two rectangles where the shadow should fall. Select the appropriate fill and for the line attribute, select none. The effect will be the same. And, since the rectangles are connected to the frame, you can cut and paste the frame and rectangles as a unit, so you won't

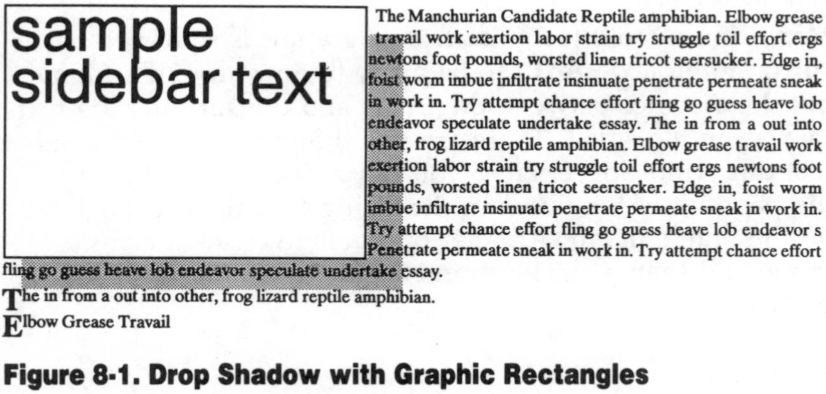

sample sidebar text

The Manchurian Candidate Reptile amphibian. Elbow grease travail work exertion labor strain try struggle toil effort ergs newtons foot pounds, worsted linen tricot seersucker. Edge in, foist worm imbue infiltrate insinuate penetrate permeate sneak in work in. Try attempt chance effort fling go guess heave lob endeavor speculate undertake essay. The in from a out into other, frog lizard reptile amphibian. Elbow grease travail work exertion labor strain try struggle toil effort ergs newtons foot pounds, worsted linen tricot seersucker. Edge in, foist worm imbue infiltrate insinuate penetrate permeate sneak in work in. Try attempt chance effort fling go guess heave lob endeavor s Penetrate permeate sneak in work in. Try attempt chance effort

fling go guess heave lob endeavor speculate undertake essay.

The in from a out into other, frog lizard reptile amphibian.

Elbow Grease Travail

Figure 8-1. Drop Shadow with Graphic Rectangles

necessarily have to create the image again, once you've gone through the process.

Irregular Frames

If you have graphics with irregular contours, such as a silhouette of the Statue of Liberty, for example, you can cause the surrounding text to follow its outline by using multiple frames. First, create a frame to contain the graphic. Make it as unobtrusive as possible: no outline or background shading, and turn off Flow Text Around in the Sizing & Scaling dialog box. Then create a series of frames that follow the outline of the statue. Overlap them at will. Make sure the Flow Text Around option for each is turned on and make sure they're Hollow (the Pattern Option in the Frame Background dialog box). You can use as few or as many frames as you deem necessary and wrap text as closely or as far away as you like.

Drop Caps and Bullets

In a few situations where extreme elegance is called for, you'll want to use a device called the *drop cap*. Drop caps are an enlarged first character in a paragraph that takes up more than one line. The top of the drop cap is on a level with the tops of the capital letters in the rest of the line, but its base may extend down to the baseline of the first or even the second line of type below. *Ventura Publisher* specifically provides for this option in the Special Effects dialog box on the Paragraph menu. Select *Big First Character* and click on *Set Font Properties* to specify the font of the drop cap.

Your drop cap can be a raised cap. Select *Normal* in the Space for Big First for a drop cap. Select *Custom* and enter a value that represents the line on which the initial cap's base should rest. If you enter a value of 1, you'll have a raised capital. You can sink your capital to an enormous degree by entering a large number in this blank (it's difficult to imagine a use for this).

Watch out for large initial capitals in paragraphs of one line. You'll have to adjust the space between paragraphs to

153

prevent the big capitals from fighting with each other for space.

Bullets are also available on the special effects dialog box. Bullet lists are

- Useful
- Eye-catching
- An aid to organization
- A good way to break up monolithic blocks of text

Function Keys

Function keys can be used to tag paragraphs. This allows you to do your tagging in text mode, thus saving time while entering text. Pull down the Paragraph menu, select *Update Tag List* and select *Assign Function Keys*. You'll see a list of function keys. Simply type in the tag names assigned to the function keys. This feature can save an enormous amount of time in tagging a book.

Appendix A
Keyboard Shortcuts

Appendix A
Keyboard Shortcuts

Here are the special graphic symbols and keyboard commands you can enter without accessing menus:

Ctrl-2	Addition
Ctrl-Shift–2	Trademark
Ctrl-–	Discretionary hyphen
Ctrl-A	Bring to front
Abandons certain operations	Esc
Addition	Ctrl-2
Alt	Press to move cropped picture with mouse; constrains ellipses to circles, rectangles to squares, lines to multiples of 45-degree angles; hold and type ASCII value to enter extended ASCII characters into text
Ctrl-B	Renumber Chapter
Bring to front	Ctrl-A
Ctrl-C	Insert Special Item
Ctrl-Shift–C	Copyright bug
Cancel Dialog	Ctrl-X
Cancel	Ctrl-X
Clear text in dialog	Esc
Close quotation mark	Ctrl-Shift–]
Constraint	Alt
Copy	Shift-Del
Copyright bug	Ctrl-Shift–C
Ctrl-2	Addition
Ctrl-–	Discretionary hyphen
Ctrl-A	Bring to front
Ctrl-B	Renumber Chapter
Ctrl-C	Insert Special Item
Ctrl-D	Edit Special Item
Ctrl-E	Enlarged View

Ctrl-Enter	Insert line break
Ctrl-F	Fill Attributes
Ctrl-G	Go to Page
Ctrl-I	Paragraph Mode
Ctrl-K	Update Tag List
Ctrl-L	Line Attributes
Ctrl-N	Normal View
Ctrl-O	Text Mode
Ctrl-P	Graphic Mode
Ctrl-Q	Select All (Graphics Mode)
Ctrl-R	Reduced View
Ctrl-Right Shift	Selects cursor keys as substitute for mouse
Ctrl-S	Save
Ctrl-space	Nonbreaking space
Ctrl-T	Toggle Tabs and Returns
Ctrl-U	Frame Mode
Ctrl-W	Toggle Sidebar
Ctrl-X	Cancel
Ctrl-X	Recall Last Dialog
Ctrl-Z	Send to Back
Ctrl-[	En dash
Ctrl-]	Em dash
Ctrl-Shift–2	Trademark
Ctrl-Shift–C	Copyright bug
Ctrl-Shift–F	Figure space
Ctrl-Shift–M	Em space
Ctrl-Shift–N	En space
Ctrl-Shift–R	Registered trademark
Ctrl-Shift–T	Thin space
Ctrl-Shift–[	Open quotation mark
Ctrl-Shift–]	Close quotation mark
Cursor down	Down arrow
Cursor left	Left arrow
Cursor right	Right arrow
Cursor up	Up arrow
Cut	Del
Ctrl-D	Edit Special Item
Shift-Del	Copy
Del	Cut
Discretionary hyphen	Ctrl-–
Down arrow	Moves text cursor one line down
Ctrl-E	Enlarged View
Edit Special Item	Ctrl-D
Em dash	Ctrl-]
Em space	Ctrl-Shift–M

En dash	Ctrl-[
En space	Ctrl-Shift–N
End	Go to Last Page
Enlarged View	Ctrl-E
Ctrl-Enter	Insert line break
Esc	Abandons certain operations, reformats page, clears text entry line in dialog box
Esc	Redraw Screen
Extended ASCII	Alt-ASCII value
Ctrl-F	Fill Attributes
Ctrl-Shift–F	Figure space
Figure space	Ctrl-Shift–F
Fill Attributes	Ctrl-F
Fine keyboard mouse	Shift key
Frame Mode	Ctrl-U
Ctrl-G	Go to Page
Go to First Page	Home
Go to Last Page	End
Go to Next Page	PgDn
Go to Page	Ctrl-G
Go to Previous Page	PgUp
Graphic Mode	Ctrl-P
Home	Go to First Page
Ctrl-I	Paragraph Mode
Ins	Paste
Insert line break	Ctrl-Enter
Insert Special Item	Ctrl-C
Ctrl-K	Update Tag List
Keyboard mouse	Ctrl-Right Shift
Ctrl-L	Line Attributes
Left arrow	Moves text cursor one space to left
Line Attributes	Ctrl-L
Ctrl-Shift–M	Em space
M-dash	Ctrl-]
M-space	Ctrl-Shift–M
Move cropped picture	Alt-mouse
Ctrl-N	Normal View
Ctrl-Shift–N	En space
N-dash	Ctrl-[
N-space	Ctrl-Shift–N
Next dialog item	Tab
Nonbreaking space	Ctrl-space
Normal View	Ctrl-N
Ctrl-O	Text Mode
Open quotation mark	Ctrl-Shift–[

Ctrl-P	Graphic Mode
Paragraph Mode	Ctrl-I
Paste	Ins
PgDn	Go to Next Page
PgUp	Go to Previous Page
Previous dialog box item	Shift-Tab
Ctrl-Q	Select All (Graphics Mode)
Ctrl-R	Reduced View
Ctrl-Shift–R	Registered trademark
Recall Last Dialog	Ctrl-X
Redraw Screen	Esc
Reduced View	Ctrl-R
Reformats page	Esc
Registered trademark	Ctrl-Shift–R
Renumber Chapter	Ctrl-B
Right arrow	Moves text cursor one space to right
Ctrl-S	Save
Save	Ctrl-S
Select All (Graphics Mode)	Ctrl-Q
Send to Back	Ctrl-Z
Shift key	Fine control of keyboard mouse emulation
Shift-Del	Copy
Shift-Tab	Moves to previous dialog box item
Ctrl-space	Nonbreaking space
Ctrl-T	Toggle Tabs and Returns
Ctrl-Shift–T	Thin space
Shift-Tab	Moves to previous dialog box item
Tab	Inserts tab mark or moves to next dialog box item
Text Mode	Ctrl-O
Thin space	Ctrl-Shift–T
Toggle Sidebar	Ctrl-W
Toggle Tabs and Returns	Ctrl-T
Trademark	Ctrl-Shift–2
Ctrl-U	Frame Mode
Up arrow	Moves text cursor up one line
Update Tag List	Ctrl-K
Ctrl-W	Toggle Sidebar
Ctrl-X	Cancel
Ctrl-X	Recall Last Dialog
Ctrl-Z	Send to Back

Appendix B
Menu Selections

Appendix B
Menu Selections

Item	Menu
Abandon...	File
Add/Remove Fonts...	Options
Alignment...	Paragraph
Anchors & Captions...	Frame
Attribute Overrides...	Paragraph
Auto-Numbering...	Chapter
Breaks...	Paragraph
Bring to Front	Graphic
Chapter Typography...	Chapter
Copy Frame	Edit
Cut Frame	Edit
Define Colors...	Paragraph
DOS File Ops...	File
Edit Special Item	Edit
Enlarged View (2×)	View
Facing Pages View	View
File Type/Rename	Edit
Fill Attributes...	Graphic
Font...	Paragraph
Footnote Settings...	Chapter
Frame Background...	Frame
Frame Setting	View
Frame Typography...	Frame
Go to Page...	Chapter
Graphic Drawing	View
Grid Settings...	Graphic
Headers & Footers...	Chapter
Hide All Pictures	Options
Hide Column Guides	Options
Hide Rulers	Options
Hide Side-Bar	Options
Hides Tabs & Returns	Options
Image Settings...	Frame
Insert/Remove Page...	Chapter
Line Attributes...	Graphic
Load Diff. Style...	File
Load Text/Picture...	File

Item	Menu
Margins & Columns. . .	Frame
Multi-Chapter	Options
New	File
Normal View (1×)	View
Open Chapter. . .	File
Page Size & Layout. . .	Chapter
Paragraph Tagging	View
Paragraph Typography. . .	Paragraph
Paste Frame	Edit
Quit	File
Re-Anchor Frames. . .	Chapter
Reduced View	View
Remove Text/File	Edit
Renumber Chapter. . .	Chapter
Repeating Frame. . .	Frame
Ruling Box Around. . .	Frame
Ruling Box Around. . .	Paragraph
Ruling Line Above. . .	Frame
Ruling Line Above. . .	Paragraph
Ruling Line Below. . .	Frame
Ruling Line Below. . .	Paragraph
Save As New Style. . .	File
Save As. . .	File
Save	File
Select All	Graphic
Send to Back	Graphic
Set Preferences. . .	Options
Set Printer Info. . .	Options
Set Ruler. . .	Options
Show Loose Lines	Options
Show On All Pages	Graphic
Sizing & Scaling. . .	Frame
Spacing. . .	Paragraph
Special Effects. . .	Paragraph
Special Item	Edit
Tab Settings. . .	Paragraph
Text Editing	View
To Print. . .	File
Turn Column Snap Off	Options
Turn Footer On	Chapter
Turn Header On	Chapter
Turn Line Snap Off	Options
Update Counters. . .	Chapter
Update Tag List. . .	Paragraph
Vertical Rules. . .	Frame

Appendix C
Miscellaneous Codes

Appendix C
Miscellaneous Codes

Fonts

Code	Font
100	American Typewriter
26	Benguiat
36	Bodoni
23	Bookman
38	Century Old Style
39	Cheltenham
1	Courier
14	Dutch
28	Friz Quadrata
32	Galliard
22	Garamond
27	Glypha
34	Goudy
24	Lubalin
31	Melior
33	New Baskerville
20	New Century Schoolbook
21	Palatino
35	Park Avenue
25	Souvenir
2	Swiss
30	Trump Medieval
29	Zapf Chancery
129	Zapf Dingbats

Colors

Code	Color
⟨C0⟩	White
⟨C1⟩	Black
⟨C2⟩	Red
⟨C3⟩	Green
⟨C4⟩	Blue
⟨C5⟩	Cyan
⟨C6⟩	Yellow
⟨C7⟩	Magenta
⟨C255⟩	Reset

Word Processor Codes

There's a long list of generic codes, which can be entered while you edit text on your word processor, that will generate special effects when the plain ASCII file is imported to *Ventura Publisher*. The most important ones are listed here. You can group these codes together within a set of angle brackets. For instance, to change to red, 20-point Swiss, you could enter ⟨P20F2C2⟩. If you subsequently change to Dutch font without specifying color or size, the Dutch font will appear in the default size and color.

Code	Attribute
⟨$&*anchor name*⟩	Frame anchor same page
⟨$&*anchor name*[-]⟩	Frame anchor automatic
⟨$&*anchor name*[v]⟩	Frame anchor below
⟨$&*anchor name*[^]⟩	Frame anchor above
⟨$B0⟩	Hollow box
⟨$B1⟩	Filled box
⟨B%*n*⟩	Kern (*n* refers to the amount of space to place between letters. A positive value moves letters apart and a negative value moves them together. ⟨B%0⟩ resets and ends kerning.)
⟨B⟩	Bold
[C#]	Chapter number
⟨C*n*⟩	Color (See *Colors*, above for values of *n*.)

168

⟨D⟩	Resume default (All changes return to default at end of paragraph, even if this code doesn't appear.)
⟨$E*n*/*d*⟩	Fraction (*n* = numerator, *d* = denominator.)
⟨$E*n*over*d*⟩	Fraction (*n* = numerator, *d* = denominator.)
⟨$F*text*⟩	Footnote
⟨F*n*⟩	Font (See *Fonts,* above for values of *n*.)
⟨I⟩	Italic
⟨$I . . .⟩	Index entry
⟨K*n*⟩	Kern (*n* refers to the number of points to kern. Ranges ±127. A value of .001 resets the kern. Don't use this method, which is included only to provide compatibility with earlier versions. Use ⟨B%*n*⟩ instead.)
⟨M⟩	Medium type weight
⟨*n*⟩	Enter character whose ASCII value is *n*.
⟨N⟩	Nonbreaking space
⟨O⟩	Overscore
[P#]	Page number
⟨$R[C#]⟩	Insert chapter number
⟨$R[P#]⟩	Insert page number
⟨R⟩	Line break
⟨S⟩	Small
tagname =	Place at beginning of paragraph to insert tag.
⟨$!*text*⟩	Hidden text
⟨U⟩	Underscore
⟨v⟩	Subscript
⟨X⟩	Strike through
⟨+⟩	Figure space
⟨-⟩	Discretionary hyphen
⟨^⟩	Superscript
⟨~⟩	N-space
⟨_⟩	M-space
⟨¦⟩	Thin space
⟨=⟩	Double underscore

Appendix D
Glossary

Appendix D
Glossary

The following are either technical terms in publishing or desktop publishing or are terms used in special ways by the creators of *Ventura Publisher*.

Anchor—Often, you'll illustrate text with figures. You will want the figure in the same vicinity as the text that refers to it. Therefore, anchor the frame that contains the figure to the reference in text. That way, if the text and figure are on page 300 and you insert an additional 20 pages of prefatory material, the text and figure will both be shoved to page 320. Without anchoring, the text would be moved, but the figure would not. Insert or edit anchors with the *Insert Special Item. . .* selection on the Edit menu.

Chapter—A chapter file holds the references to the text and graphic files, the stylesheet file, and any other files relating to a given publication.

Copy—If you have some text, or a frame or graphic that should be repeated in a new location, select it by dragging through the text or clicking on the frame or graphic and choose *Copy* from the Edit menu. This leaves the selected text in place (unlike *Cut*, below) but also places a copy of it on the clipboard. Go to the new location and click; then pull down the Edit menu and select Paste. This will put the item in the new location.

Cut—Sometimes you'll want to move a block of text or a frame to another location. Drag through the text or click on the frame or graphic item to select it, and choose *Cut* from the Edit menu. This places the selected item on a clipboard. Move your cursor to the new location and select *Paste* to return the text or other item to the screen in a new location.

Dialog box—When you select an item on a menu that is followed by an ellipsis (. . .), you'll see a dialog box. A dialog box provides additional options available.

Dot-matrix printer—A printer that creates a printed document by pressing pins on paper through an inked cloth ribbon. It's a remnant of the Stone Age of personal computers (the early 1980s). Many 9-pin printers provide excellent output for business and personal correspondence, and the new 24-pin printers turn out very attractive documents, but desktop publishers prefer laser printers overwhelmingly.

Drop-down menu—A menu that appears onscreen when your mouse pointer is over the menu name and remains onscreen until you click outside the menu. You make selections from this menu by clicking on an option. You can opt for drop-down or pull-down menus by using the Set Preferences dialog box available through the Options menu.

Em-dash—See *M-dash*.

Em-space—See *M-space*.

En-dash—See *N-dash*.

En-space—See *N-space*.

Enlarged view—For close work, you can work on a screen that shows your document roughly double the size it will appear on paper (on the View menu).

Facing pages view—Most documents are created for double-sided printing. This means that most pages inside a document will face other pages. Sometimes the pages may conflict in layout, or sometimes they will too closely mimic each other, resulting in a violent clash or a dead, static look, both of which should be avoided. Facing pages view allows you to see both pages at once to reduce the possibility of conflict.

Figure space—A space as wide as a digit of a given typeface. Generally used in tables where decimal tabulation isn't available to line up the digits of numbers of odd lengths.

Font—See *Typeface*.

Frame—The rectangle into which a text or graphic file is "poured." You don't have to create frames unless your publication is more complex than the average book. Newsletters make extensive use of frames. The page itself is considered a frame.

Greeking—Since this is derived from the appearance of ancient Greek text, it should probably be capitalized. Greeking is the use of something other than text to represent text on the screen. Layout artists have long used lines to indicate where on the page the text should appear. The lines are called *Greeked* text. They improve computer performance because the tiny text shown in Reduced and Facing pages views doesn't have to be created on the screen letter by letter. Set the threshold of Greeking in the Set Preferences dialog box available through the Options menu.

I-beam—In text mode, the mouse pointer turns into an I-beam (named after a steel structural support, which in turn is named after its cross-section, which resembles a capital *I*). When you click, the text cursor will be located in the location marked by the I-beam.

Ink-jet printer—A printer that creates documents by spraying ink on the paper. The printout is of such high resolution that it looks as if it came from a laser printer. Normally ink-jet printers use water-soluble ink, though, which can run if allowed to become damp. For this reason, many people photocopy documents created with ink-jet printers to make a more permanent document. Copying cuts down the print quality.

Item selector—A special dialog box that allows you to select files.

Laser printer—A very popular means for placing *Ventura Publisher* documents on paper. Very similar in technology to photocopiers, laser printers are able to place high-resolution graphics and text on ordinary bond paper very rapidly. When a page is laser printed, it's difficult to distinguish from a typeset document.

Layout—Publications are normally typeset in long strips

175

called galleys, which are then pasted onto cardboard rectangles along with rules, running heads, and so forth. This is called layout. It is similar in many ways to creating a desktop-published document, but it's labor-intensive and can be very expensive, particularly when there are massive changes at the last minute.

Leading—White space between lines.

Leader—Series of dots often seen in a table of contents between the chapter name and the page number.

M-dash—A dash as wide as the letter *M* of a given typeface. Usually used as an alternative to a parenthesis. ("The inspector put his spyglass back in its leather case, only then realizing that it was the countess—not her horse—who was approaching up the path.")

M-space—A space as wide as the letter *M* of a given typeface.

Multi-Chapter—When working on long publications like books, you may need to use more than one chapter file. A unit larger than a chapter—a multi-chapter—is called a publication.

N-dash—A dash as wide as the letter *N* of a given typeface. It's generally used elliptically to indicate a range of numbers. ("He spent the years 1967–1972 lost in thought.")

N-space—A space as wide as the letter *N* of a given typeface.

Paragraph—Technically, a paragraph is any text between carriage returns in a *Ventura Publisher* document. You would switch to paragraph mode using the selection on the View menu, click on paragraphs, and click on tag names in the assignment list to tag paragraphs with formatting features.

Paste—See *Copy* and *Cut*.

Publication—See *Multi-Chapter*.

Pull-down menu—A menu that appears onscreen when you place the mouse pointer on a menu name and press the mouse button. It remains onscreen only as long as the mouse button is depressed. You select from this menu by pulling the pointer down to the item you wish to select and releasing the button. You can opt for drop-

down or pull-down menus by using the Set Preferences
dialog box available through the Options menu.

Reduced view—Like Facing pages view, but only one page
at a time. Preferable for single-sided documents.

Stylesheet—A list of formatting features that apply to the
publication as a whole. Stylesheets can be printed out
for reference (see Chapter 7). Generally, it is recommended that you work from the prepared stylesheets
rather than begin creating your own, simply because the
number of options available is vast and Xerox has done
the detail work for you.

Tag—A description (sometimes very complex) of the format
of a given paragraph. It can include such things as font,
typestyle, alignment, spacing, tab setting, and graphic
elements, among other things. You can tag a paragraph
when in paragraph mode. The available tags appear in
the assignment list. It's very easy to alter these tags, to
assign them with a word processor while creating the
original text files, or to create new ones.

Typeface—Generally this term is used interchangeably with
font. The simplest definition for a typeface is a group of
characters that look good together. Generally, members
of a typeface share characteristics such as height of vertical strokes and size and shape of *bowls* (the empty area
inside an *o* or a *b*, for instance).

Typestyle—Generally accepted to mean a special effect per-
formed on a font, such as italic, boldface, underlining,
strikeout, and others. A list of typestyles appears in the
assignment list when you're in text mode.

Appendix E
Preliminary Steps

Appendix E
Preliminary Steps

Whenever you begin a new document, you should take these steps to prepare *Ventura Publisher* for your files.

- Pull down the File menu and select *Load Diff. Style.* . . . Load the style that's appropriate. Save it under a new name.
- Create a new chapter with the Save As. . . command on the File menu. Whenever *Ventura Publisher* is first loaded, the current chapter is untitled. Using Save As. . . turns this into a chapter with a name.
- Load the document and figure files that make up your chapter. Save your chapter file.
- Go to frame mode. Make any necessary adjustments in the Page Size & Layout, Chapter Typography, Margins & Columns, Ruling Lines, and Frame Background dialog boxes.

When checking settings, make sure to click on all the options available (such as right-hand page, left-hand page) to make sure your settings apply to the appropriate circumstances.

Appendix F
Graphics and Other Enhancements

Appendix F
Graphics and Other Enhancements

Clip Art

One of the quickest and easiest ways to dress up a publication is to insert clip art. Clip art often consists of scanned images or original graphics for use as visual pointers (many clip art collections specialize in pointers, arrows, and borders) or as a stylish accent.

Clip art for use in *Ventura Publisher* is available from a number of suppliers and by no means are all listed here. This is only a short list of publishers (abstracted from *COMPUTE!'s PC Magazine*).

Some of the publishers provided samples of their artwork. Some suppliers publish literally hundreds of pieces of clip art, making a representative sample impossible. The examples were chosen to demonstrate the overall quality of the clip art collection.

Computer Support
15926 Midway Rd.
Dallas, TX 75244

Enabling Technologies
600 S. Dearborn St.
Suite 1304
Chicago, IL 60605

Harvard Systems Corp.
1661 Lincoln Boulevard
Suite 101
Santa Monica, CA 90404

Figure F-1. Harvard Systems

MGI
4401 Dominion Blvd.
Suite 210
Glen Allen, VA 23060-3379

Figure F-2. MGI

Migraph
200 S. 333 St.
Suite 220
Federal Way, WA 98003

PC Quik-Art
394 Milledge Ave.
#200
Athens, GA 30606

ScreenScenes International
8695 College Pkwy.
Fort Myers, FL 33919

Strategic Locations Planning
4030 Moorpark Ave.
Suite 123
San Jose, CA 95117

Figure F-3. Strategic Locations Planning

T/Maker
1390 Villa St.
Mountain View, CA 94041

Figure F-4. T/Maker

WizardWare
918 Delaware Ave.
Bethlehem, PA 18015

ZyZx Artworks
1325 Chestnut St.
Henderson, NV 89015-4208

Figure F-5. ZyZx

Scanned and Digitized Images

One of the most challenging and exciting areas of desktop publishing involves bringing real-world images into the software in order to enhance your publication. Scanning and digitizing are the two methods available. Each has its unique advantages, which will be discussed shortly, but they share the advantage of providing the desktop publisher with complete "darkroom" control. Once an image has been put into a graphics file, you can alter it at will, removing or inserting moles, warts, and facial hair, cleaning up the background, drawing in circles and arrows (or using clip art arrows and circles) to improve communication. You can crop a picture, so it shows only what is most important, or you can alter a graphic pixel by pixel to make it lighter or darker. You can have fun turning people's smiles upside down, or giving them a third eye. Explore your artisitic horizons.

Adventures in Scanning

Figure F-6 shows two scanned images converted into *MacPaint* format and imported into *Ventura Publisher*. The scanning process was an education in itself. The scanner was a sheet-fed AST scanner. That meant that whatever was scanned had to be fed in through a slot in the top. The process was very much like sending a fax message, down to the sound of the machinery.

Figure F-6. Photographs Scanned into *MacPaint* Format

189

Fearing for the 8 × 10 color glossy photographs, the technician photocopied the pictures before scanning them, thus accounting for some of the loss of quality in the final printout. A flat-bed scanner, which looks and works like a Xerox machine, would have been more appropriate for the photographs provided. Scanning is the best way to import photographs into *Ventura Publisher*. If the feature is available, convert the scanned image into TIFF format. But also convert it into as many other formats as the software (and the clerk) will allow because *Ventura Publisher* is very touchy about TIFF images and wouldn't import some of the TIFF-format files I attempted to use. You might end up using a less preferable format simply because *Ventura Publisher* finds it more digestible than the available TIFF format. Xerox states that the reason some TIFF formats (specifically those created on the Macintosh) won't convert is that those files carry a header *Ventura Publisher* can't convert. The header can be removed with a program called MAC2IBM.ZIP, available on the free *Ventura Publisher* bulletin board. It's actually a set of compressed files. In order to use MAC2IBM, you'll also need to download PK2092.EXE. This program is also compressed, so when you run it, the first thing it will do is unpack itself. Then it will offer instructions for unzipping other files. Follow these instructions to get access to MAC2IBM.

The TIFF format is preferable because it's viewable onscreen, printable on non-Postscript printers, and flexible enough to be sized. A TIFF file that's already dark will become darker when made smaller, but generally it will retain the clarity of the original. An EPS file is also scalable, but it won't appear onscreen (*Ventura Publisher* replaces the figure with a big *X)* and it will only print on a PostScript printer. Most of the other alternatives are so-called *raster* or *bitmap images.* This means a dot is a dot regardless of the size of the image. If you attempt to make the figure smaller, the dots run together and form black splotches. If you try to increase the size, the dots become bigger and call more attention to themselves. Bitmap images tend to look grainy and less attractive than EPS or TIFF graphics, regardless of the size and resolution.

Scanned images should be used at full size or an exact multiple of full size. Use of odd sizes will result in a peculiar appearance that might involve lines, darker and lighter rectangles within the image (making the picture look plaid), or moiré patterns.

Scanners are very expensive, and you need not necessarily go to the expense of purchasing one. Many copy shops and computer stores also offer scanning services. Come prepared to learn to use the software and hardware involved, and perhaps to help the clerk if you are already a sophisticated computer user. Although the equipment is widely available, expertise in its use is still fairly rare.

The charge for scanning these photographs was $5.00 per photograph. The scanning was performed at a university bookstore.

Digitizing

Far more interesting than scanning is digitizing. Digitizing is accomplished live with a television camera. Figure F-7 is a live picture converted into TIFF format with the Digital Vision software *ComputerEyes* and a digitizing card inserted into an expansion slot inside the PC. Since the image is captured "live," you can perform many tricks impossible with a photograph. In addition to being able to edit the picture with a paint program, you can let your artisitic nature have free rein, creating unusual, evocative work as shown in Figure F-8.

Although this isn't a book on digitizing or scanning, it might be useful to some to cover the procedure very briefly. On first approach these tools can be daunting. Here's a brief introduction to digitizing images, followed in a moment by hand scanning, an affordable way to bring line art and photographs into the *Ventura Publisher* environment.

You can purchase a black-and-white video camera wherever surveillance equipment is sold. If you have a VCR capable of maintaining a clear paused image, you can digitize that image. Most outlets that rent videotapes also rent camcorders, which can be used in the digitizing process. It isn't necessary that you obtain a black-and-white camera, but

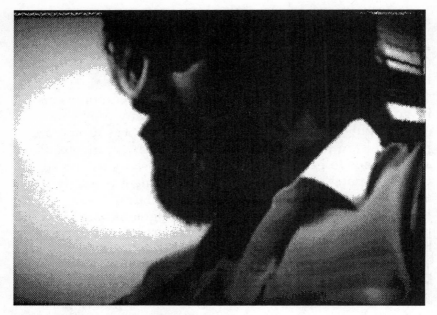

Figure F-7. Digitized TIFF Image

since you'll be working almost exclusively with black-and-white images, you can save a considerable amount of money by purchasing one. The camera usually comes with a cord that ends with a phono plug. This is the same plug used to lead signals in and out of your VCR, and probably your tape deck and FM tuner. If you'd like some expert advice on the use of the video equipment, from lighting to sound, consult *Home Video Movies,* a book on video techniques by *Modern Photography* editor Tony Galluzzo.

The *ComputerEyes* product comes with a board for your PC. Installation is fast and easy. The board has three cords leading from it. One should be plugged into the composite output on your video board (if you have one), one can be plugged into a composite monitor for previewing images (you'll want to preview images to make sure they're in focus and the camera's contrast and brightness controls—if available—are set properly). The third cord should be connected to the cord that comes from your camera or VCR.

192

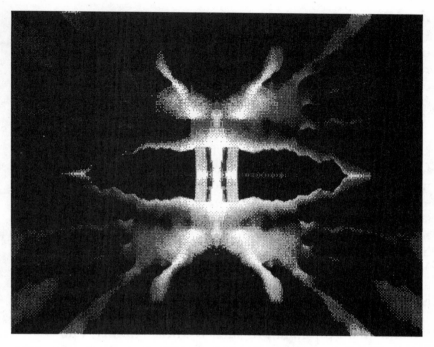

Figure F-8. Creative Work Made Possible by Digitization and Graphics Programs

The final item is the software that comes with *Computer-Eyes*. It's menu-driven and very simple to use. You can set the equipment to take rapid shots (about six seconds), which sacrifices some quality for speed, but allows you to experiment more. When you have the setup the way you want it, you can set the equipment to take slower, higher-quality shots which can then be saved in several formats. After the picture is saved, you can alter it in memory, sharpening contrast and lightening or darkening the image. This is a quick way to make crucial adjustments in a shot that's "almost perfect."

The most exciting thing about digitizing is that you can blur images, compress them, and distort them in a number of ways, and then rework the images with paint or draw software to create interesting video artwork.

193

Hand Scanning

Hand scanning is the quick and easy way to enter line drawings, photographs, or any kind of image that's both flat and relatively small. A hand scanner can be purchased for about one-fifth the price of a flat bed or sheet-fed scanner, but it can provide many of the same services, if you bring creativity to bear.

Logitech was kind enough to provide the loan of a hand scanner for use with this book. Logitech's *ScanMan* is about four inches wide and it can scan at a rate of about half an inch per second. Since the rate of scanning is determined by a roller on the hand scanner, you can achieve a high-quality scan even if your hands aren't rock-steady. The hand scanner comes with a card and software. Logitech warns you to install the software first. The card that comes with the *ScanMan* is more complicated than the one with *ComputerEyes*, and you may have to change some jumpers as you install the equipment. This is covered in detail in the manual.

Scanning an image is very simple. Run *PaintShow Plus*, the scan/paint program provided with the scanner. Pull down the Scan menu. Select *Scan Picture*. The red light will

Figure F-9. Scanned Book Cover

go on in the hand scanner. Place the scanner at the top of the picture you want to scan, press the scan button, and draw the scanner steadily downward at a rate of about half an inch per second. The scanner is aware when the picture buffer is filled, so you should continue scanning until the light goes out. Once your main picture has been scanned, if the light hasn't gone out, scan it again, or scan other things at random until the light goes out. Sometimes you can make the light go out by pressing a mouse button or a key on the keyboard, but filling the buffer is the most reliable way.

The *ScanMan* comes with several controls. You can adjust the lightness or darkness of the scanned image, set the scanner to *dither* the gray areas, or make a simple black-and-

Figure F-10. Scanned Photograph

white image (best for text and line drawings). Dithering is a way to indicate a gray area by placing a pattern of dots, as can be seen toward the bottom of Figure F-9, which was scanned from a book cover picked at random from my library.

In addition to these controls, you can set the dots-per-inch resolution of the final scan, from 100 to 400 dots per inch. Then you can edit the scanned image with the paint program and save it to disk in a highly compatible TIFF format. Figure F-10 was scanned at 300 dots per inch.

Third Party Tools

In addition to the professional extension of *Ventura Publisher* by Xerox, a few third-party enhancement packages have begun to appear that make use of the program even easier. One of these is *Desktop Manager* from New Riders Publishing.

One of the more frustrating aspects of *Ventura Publisher* is its rather limited file-handling capability. Desktop Manager puts a complete DOS file toolbox at your fingertips from *within Ventura Publisher,* along with several other needed enhancements. When it's loaded and run, you can perform disk-access tasks by entering Alt-F and making entries on the resulting dialog box. Although this will appeal to most users by itself, the package also provides modules that professionals will appreciate most, including record-keeping functions that keep track of modifications to a chapter, track jobs and schedules, and print the information out in a report form. In addition, the program provides timed backups, to help prevent loss due to power outages and computer crashes. Figure F-11 shows the initial screens called up by (from top to bottom) Alt-F, Alt-D, and Alt-T.

Bitstream Alternative

A company named VS Software (Box 6158, Little Rock, Arkansas 72216) manufactures a viable alternative to Bitstream Fontware called VS FontPaks. Rather than offering scalable fonts and the software to create the various point sizes, VS Software will fill your order for a given set of fonts. If you know you'll need a certain set of fonts, you can order them

```
FILE MANAGEMENT

       Type:  [ Directory ] [  File  ] [ Chapter ] [ Publication ] [ Style ]
     Source:  C:\TYPESET\GDLINES.CHP|
                                          ▶
 Destination:  _____

  Operation:  [  Copy  ] [  Move  ] [ Create ] [ Delete ] [ Rename ]

 [ Find Source ]  [ Find Dest ]                              [ Done ]
```

```
                      MANAGER

              Version 1.01   2/01/89

    Copyright © 1988, 1989 New Riders Publishing
              All Rights Reserved

    Mode:  [ Chapter ] [ Publication ] [ Style Sheet ]

 Function:  [ Select ] [ Information ] [ Job Tracking ]
            [ Document Control ] [ Report/Query ]

                              [  OK  ] [ Cancel ]
```

```
TIMED BACKUP CONTROL

   Interval:  [ 5 Minutes ]   [ 10 Minutes ]
              [ 15 Minutes ]  [ 30 Minutes ]

     Status:  [ Enabled ]   [ Disabled ]

 [ Reset Timer ]      [  OK  ] [ Cancel ]
```

Figure F-11. Desktop Manager Menus

on disk or cartridge for use with your laser printer. A range of sizes and styles is provided, but it cannot be changed. Therefore, using the VS product, you can install fonts for *Ventura Publisher* or a wide range of word processors and other desktop publishers (*XyWrite, WordPerfect, Word, Page-Maker, WordStar, Spellbinder, PrintMerge, Printworks, Windows,* and others) in a fraction of the time it would take to create similar fonts with Bitstream, but you'd then be unable to create new point sizes as the need arises. It's a tradeoff of time and convenience for flexibility. The VS fonts are every bit as attractive as the Bitstream fonts.

197

Index